ORTHO'S All About

Windows,
Doors, and Skylights

Meredith® Books
Des Moines, Iowa

Ortho® Books
An imprint of Meredith® Books

Ortho's All About Windows, Doors, and Skylights
Editor: Larry Johnston
Contributing Writer: Jeff Abugel
Art Director: Tom Wegner
Assistant Art Director: Harijs Priekulis
Copy Chief: Catherine Hamrick
Copy and Production Editor: Terri Fredrickson
Book Production Managers: Pam Kvitne,
    Marjorie J. Schenkelberg
Contributing Copy Editor: Steve Hallam
Technical Proofreader: Ray Kast
Contributing Proofreaders: Dan Degen, Colleen Johnson,
    JoEllyn Witke
Indexer: Barbara L. Klein
Electronic Production Coordinator: Paula Forest
Editorial and Design Assistants: Kathleen Stevens,
    Karen Schirm

**Additional Editorial Contributions from
    Art Rep Services**
Director: Chip Nadeau
Designer: lk Design
Illustrator: Shawn Wallace

Meredith® Books
Editor in Chief: James D. Blume
Design Director: Matt Strelecki
Managing Editor: Gregory H. Kayko
Executive Ortho Editor: Larry Erickson

Director, Retail Sales and Marketing: Terry Unsworth
Director, Sales, Special Markets: Rita McMullen
Director, Sales, Premiums: Michael A. Peterson
Director, Sales, Retail: Tom Wierzbicki
Director, Sales, Home & Garden Centers: Ray Wolf
Director, Book Marketing: Brad Elmitt
Director, Operations: George A. Susral
Director, Production: Douglas M. Johnston

Vice President, General Manager: Jamie L. Martin

Meredith Publishing Group
President, Publishing Group: Christopher M. Little
Vice President, Finance & Administration: Max Runciman

Meredith Corporation
Chairman and Chief Executive Officer: William T. Kerr

Chairman of the Executive Committee: E.T. Meredith III

Photographers
    (Photographers credited may retain copyright ©
    to the listed photographs.)
L = Left, R = Right, C = Center, B = Bottom, T = Top
King Au: 78–79
Ross Chapple: 79BR
Hopkins Associates: 80, 89BL
Hy-Lite Products, Inc.: 52
Inside Out Studio: 13, 23
Jenifer Jordan: 32, 48–49, 81B
ODL, Inc.: 5BR, 7, 81T, 81C, 89R
Pella Corporation: 4–5, 53T, 53B
D. Randolph: 49BR
Rick Taylor: 41
Weather Shield Manufacturing, Inc.: 50, 66, 67BL, 67BC,
    67BR, 72

All of us at Ortho® Books are dedicated to providing you
with the information and ideas you need to enhance your
home and garden. We welcome your comments and
suggestions about this book. Write to us at:
    Meredith Corporation
    Ortho Books
    1716 Locust St.
    Des Moines, IA 50309–3023

If you would like more information on other Ortho
products, call 800-225-2883 or visit us at www.ortho.com

Note to the Readers: Due to differing conditions, tools,
and individual skills, Meredith Corporation assumes no
responsibility for any damages, injuries suffered, or losses
incurred as a result of following the information published
in this book. Before beginning any project, review the
instructions carefully, and if any doubts or questions remain,
consult local experts or authorities. Because codes and
regulations vary greatly, you always should check with
authorities to ensure that your project complies with all
applicable local codes and regulations. Always read and
observe all of the safety precautions provided by
manufacturers of any tools, equipment, or supplies,
and follow all accepted safety procedures.

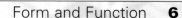

DOORS 4

WINDOWS 48

SKYLIGHTS 78

DOORS

While often taken for granted, every door in your home serves both practical and aesthetic roles. The entry door, in addition to its obvious functions, often makes an opening statement about your home, subtly setting the stage for what's inside. Interior doors provide privacy and security while further establishing the home's architectural style with their materials or finishes. Patio doors help integrate the home with the outdoor environment.

This chapter examines some of the types of doors to consider when building a home or remodeling one. You'll find a wide variety of door styles and materials on the market today; many of them can improve your home's energy efficiency, too. This chapter will help you make decisions about what types of doors to buy and show how you can install them yourself with basic carpentry skills.

Chapter 2 addresses windows for your home, and Chapter 3 gives information about skylights.

Doors play an important part in setting the style and mood of a room.

FORM AND FUNCTION

FINDING THE STYLE

Architects and designers usually give a building's entry special consideration when drawing up new blueprints. That's because doors and entries have historically made statements about what to expect inside, whether the building is a gothic cathedral, a restaurant, or a country farmhouse. Your home is no different.

Door placement makes part of the statement. A covered entry placed dead center in a two-story home with equally spaced windows and shutters looks orderly and symmetrical. The same central placement on a contemporary ranch-style house might look boring.

The door's design is important, too. Double entry doors with an arched transom would overpower a smaller ranch house, just as a country-style Dutch door would clash with a formal brick colonial facade.

You can alter the looks of your home by changing its doorways, or by planning the right doors in the blueprint stage. Take care to select entry and interior doors that suit your home's style. Mixing styles can sometimes work effectively and is more acceptable than it once was.

TRAFFIC FLOW

Placement of interior doors affects your home's livability. Doors opening against each other create awkward areas. Doorways opposing each other across a room will probably establish a traffic pattern right through the middle of it.

Whether you're looking over new house plans or planning new doors for your existing home, make sure that fully opened doors don't collide and that traffic patterns will be agreeable. Plan door placements with both function and design in mind—a door put in as an afterthought will usually appear to be just that.

WEATHER PROTECTION

Exterior doors—even those sheltered by a porch roof or protected behind a storm door—must fend off all kinds of weather. Wind, rain, and snow will find their way through your front door unless you take precautions to keep them out.

In cold or windy climates, avoid facing a door toward the prevailing winds. If this is impossible, consider shielding the entry from direct blasts of wind. Landscaping, walls, or half walls can help defend the door against the weather. In warmer parts of the country, you might be able to block the wind with a

EXTERIOR STYLES

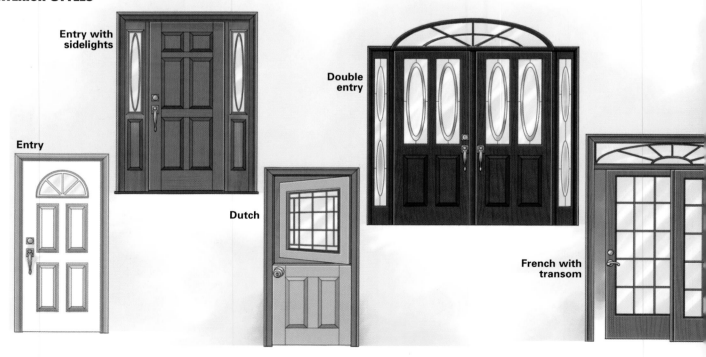

Entry with sidelights

Entry

Dutch

Double entry

French with transom

trellis and some well-established vines. A wall inside the house can shield a room from an entry-door wind blast, too. Even a half wall can be helpful since cold air sinks.

If driving wind and rain are a problem, plan for a sheltering roof of some kind over the door. Be sure to include a rain gutter or diverter so you won't have to walk through a waterfall to get to the door.

An overhanging roof above the door will also help to protect it from weathering and leaking. Doors are designed to be water- and wind-resistant, but they aren't waterproof. Allowing water to stream over or onto a door is inviting trouble.

LIGHT AND VENTILATION

Exterior doors can let light and air into a room. An entry door with a window in it—called a door light—can help brighten a dark entry area. French doors and sliding glass doors both admit plenty of light, but French doors are harder to screen than sliding doors. For the look of a traditional French door with the convenience of easy screening, consider wood sliding doors. You always need to balance added light and ventilation with safety and security considerations, too.

SECURITY

Metal doors are strong and fire-resistant. Solid-wood or solid-core exterior doors also

offer security, but the panels in some paneled doors might be easy to break through.

Sidelight windows beside a front door should be glazed with breakage-resistant plastic. The same holds true for any door lights, too.

French doors opening to a patio may look inviting to burglars. Break out one panel, reach in, and unlock the door, and they're in. Breakage-resistant glazing prevents that kind of entry, however, and better doors offer added security features such as throw bolts. All exterior doors should be equipped with dead-bolt locks.

SAFETY

Check your local code requirements for glazing material in door lights and sidelights. Safety glazing will be called for if the opening exceeds a certain size. Some choices are tempered glass, which is heat treated to break into tiny fragments instead of large, sharp shards; laminated safety glass, like that in an auto windshield; and plastic glazing.

Sidelights help set off an entry door and give it more presence. The large arched transom window over the door makes this entry even more impressive.

INTERIOR STYLES

Bifold

Three-piece patio

DOOR SIZES

■ Door dimensions are traditionally stated in feet and inches. For example, a 30-inch-wide door (2 feet, 6 inches) is called a 2-6 door, pronounced "two-six."

■ Standard door height is 6-8, or 80 inches.

■ When giving both dimensions, width comes first: 2-6×6-8.

■ Doors come in even-inch widths, generally ranging from 1-0 to 3-0; don't go shopping for a 2-7 door.

■ Exterior doors are normally 1¾ inch thick; interior ones, 1⅜ inch.

■ A front entry door is ordinarily a 3-0 door; a back entry door can be either a 3-0 or 2-8.

EXTERIOR DOORS

Ability to ward off the weather is only one of the considerations in buying an exterior door. You'll find a broad range of options in quality and materials at home centers, lumberyards, or the newer specialty window stores that major manufacturers have opened. In most cases, too, you'll get what you pay for. For instance, a top-of-the-line wood door could outperform a low-quality steel one by far in years of service, R-value, and ease of maintenance. Another decision you'll face is whether to install a prehung unit. Many of the most energy-efficient doors are sold as prehung units that you just slide into the hole in your wall. In some cases, however, you may want to install a new door in an existing jamb or build your own jamb into the wall.

CHARACTERISTICS OF EXTERIOR DOORS

■ Solid-wood or solid-core construction
■ Solid-core doors may be metal- or vinyl-clad
■ 1¾ inches thick

ANATOMY OF A DOOR

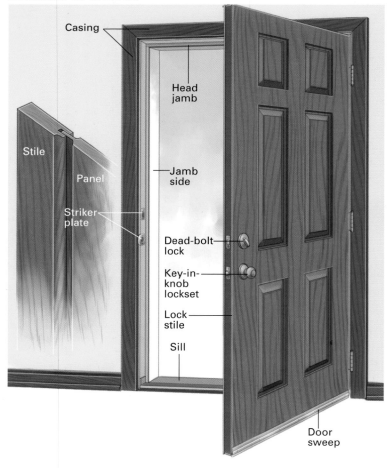

Casing

Head jamb

Stile

Panel

Jamb side

Striker plate

Dead-bolt lock

Key-in-knob lockset

Lock stile

Sill

Door sweep

WOOD DOORS

Wood has been a popular door material for centuries and remains the first choice for many who appreciate its warmth and character. Exterior wood door construction can be either solid panel or solid core.

A traditional solid-wood paneled door is made up of vertical side members, called stiles, joined by two or more horizontal rails. Stiles and rails are glued together and are usually reinforced by dowels or mortise and tenon joints. The panels fit into the spaces created, free to move to accommodate swelling or shrinkage due to varying humidity.

In a solid-core door, veneer faces cover a core of laminated wood or particleboard. The top, bottom, and edges of the core are usually solid wood to allow trimming for height and for hardware mounting.

WEATHER PROTECTION FOR WOOD DOORS: Some doors feature aluminum or vinyl cladding on the out-facing side to improve their weather resistance and durability. Claddings are available in a wide variety of colors. The wood on the inside surface is often treated with a light, clear preservative coating, over which you can apply paint or stain.

Aluminum cladding usually looks crisper and may take paint finishes better, although your best bet is to stick with the factory colors. Vinyl is better than aluminum in marine climates, where the salt air will eventually pit aluminum.

Another protective coat for wood doors is polyurethane finish, similar to paint, but more durable. These coatings are salt-resistant and stretch with the wood as it swells and contracts with changes in humidity. Some units are available with clad jambs and a polyurethane finish on the door itself—an attractive and durable combination.

OTHER MATERIALS

Steel exterior doors are frequently installed in new construction and as replacement entry doors in older homes. They are often available as prehung units and offer strength and durability. Steel doors won't warp, of course, and they don't shrink and swell with climatic changes. An insulation-filled core, coupled with magnetic weather stripping, makes these doors highly energy efficient.

Fiberglass doors, constructed much like steel ones, offer another alternative to wood.

Sliding patio doors are usually made of aluminum. Durable and attractive powder-coat and paint finishes are now available in addition to the silver mill finish that was standard years ago.

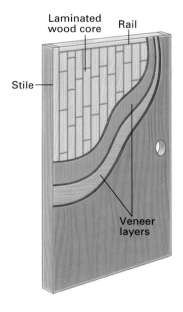

Laminated wood core

Rail

Stile

Veneer layers

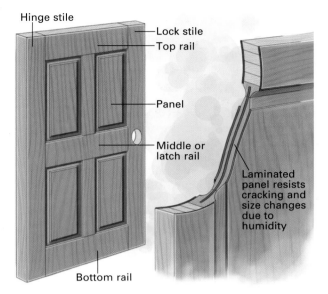

Hinge stile

Lock stile

Top rail

Panel

Middle or latch rail

Bottom rail

Laminated panel resists cracking and size changes due to humidity

Wood

Wood exterior doors are traditional, and so are their problems: the door will swell and shrink along with climatic changes. This can lead to a door that sticks in the humid season and doesn't fit tightly in the dry months. Wood exterior doors usually have solid cores. Their R-values depend on their construction. Wood doors require periodic refinishing.

Steel

Residential steel doors suggest fortresslike protection. Embossed steel covers and applied moldings give many steel doors a traditional, woodlike appearance, too. Insulation-filled steel doors can provide R-values of up to R-15. They don't change size with the season, and are fire-resistant and durable. But steel doors can be more difficult to install. You can't plane them to fit as you can a wood door, so frames must be perfectly square and plumb.

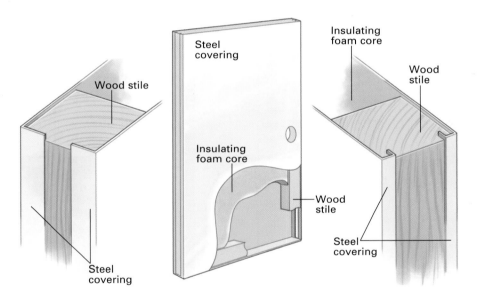

Wood stile

Steel covering

Steel covering

Steel covering

Insulating foam core

Wood stile

Steel covering

Insulating foam core

Wood stile

Wood stile

Molded fiber-reinforced plastic panel

Wood stile

Insulating foam core

Fiber-reinforced plastic covering

Fiber-reinforced plastic

The very idea of a plastic door strikes terror into the hearts of some aesthetic-minded people. But these doors can look just like wood. They are lightweight and easy to handle, too, which could soften your objections considerably if you're thinking of installing the door yourself. Insulated fiberglass doors carry R-values up to R-11, and many can be painted or stained like wood.

INTERIOR DOORS

Interior doors complement and enhance the architecture and interior style of a house, as well as meeting traffic control, environmental control, privacy, and security needs. Changing interior doors or doorways can affect the style of a home dramatically. For example, installing new decorative panel doors, French doors, or pocket doors in place of flush, hollow-core doors offers a certain way to alter a home's character and style.

When planning or changing doors, try to maintain some consistency of style. A family room with doors markedly different from those in the rest of the house may look fine if the doors fit the room's style and decor. But mixing door styles in the same space can appear haphazard and poorly planned.

While manufacturers offer numerous styles of exterior entry doors, you may not find as many choices in interior, or passage, doors. Flush, hollow-core doors with birch or mahogany faces are the norm and are widely available at lumberyards and home centers. You'll find more decorative doors with embossed hardwood or molded plastic faces there, too. You may have to special-order panel doors, French doors, and other styles.

Most interior doors are manufactured in 1⅜-inch thickness, though bifold doors are also made in 1¼- and 1⅛-inch thicknesses. Most doors are also made in standard 6-foot-8-inch heights; widths range from 1 foot to 3 feet in increments of 2 inches.

CHARACTERISTICS OF INTERIOR DOORS

■ Hollow-core, solid-core, or wood-panel construction
■ Flush or decorative faces on nonpanel doors may be wood veneer, hardboard, or plastic
■ 1⅜ inches thick

BIFOLD, SLIDING, AND POCKET DOORS

Bifold and sliding doors are convenient for closets, pantries, laundry areas, and the like. A pocket door—one that slides into the wall when open—proves useful where a hinged door just won't work.

Bypass sliding doors are often installed where limited clearance requires a door that doesn't swing in or out when open. Commonly seen on closets, the bypass door's main drawback is that you can't have the entire opening clear. Sliding doors are usually standard 1⅜-inch-thick interior doors. Some units feature metal or plastic door panels. Metal-framed mirrored doors are available.

Bifold doors provide a clear—or nearly clear—opening, but protrude from the door frame when open. When installing bifolds in front of laundry equipment, for instance, you need to build an opening wide enough that the open doors won't hinder access to the equipment. Bifold door panels are usually 1⅛ or 1¼ inches thick. Again, metal and plastic units are available.

A pocket door affords a clear opening and doesn't extend from the frame when open. But aside from these utilitarian advantages, the pocket door—and especially a pair of them—can lend elegance as an entry to a living room, dining room, or library, for example. When planning for one, remember that the installation involves opening a hole in the wall about twice the width of the door. Pocket-door frames take standard 1⅜-inch interior doors.

OTHER CONSIDERATIONS

Think about noise control when you plan interior door installations. Hollow-core doors don't block noise as well as solid ones. This

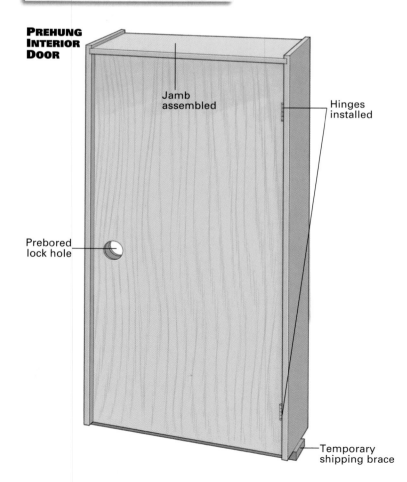

PREHUNG INTERIOR DOOR

Jamb assembled

Hinges installed

Prebored lock hole

Temporary shipping brace

Rail

Panel

Stile

Stile

Solid-wood panel

Stile

Solid-wood
Solid-wood doors are constructed of wood, normally with panel inserts. They're sturdy and attractive, and can be painted or stained.

may be important for a door leading to a laundry room or family room.

If you are replacing or adding a door between a living space and a garage, you should use a fire-resistant unit with an automatic closing device. Local building codes may specify acceptable types of doors and closers.

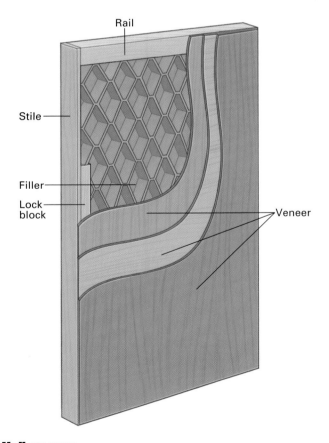

Rail

Stile

Filler

Lock block

Veneer

Hollow-core
Hollow-core doors have a cardboard honeycomb center covered with wood veneer, hardboard, or plastic. They're inexpensive and readily available.

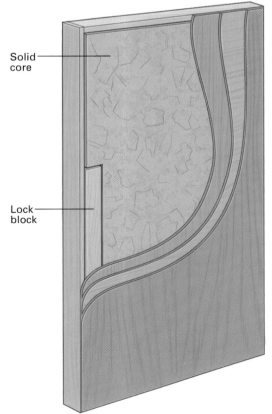

Solid core

Lock block

Solid-core
Solid-core doors are made of particleboard or laminated wood covered by wood veneer. Solid-core interior doors are sometimes hard to find.

STRUCTURAL BASICS

Framing and hanging doors takes you right to the very skeleton of your house—the framing. An understanding of house framing will prove invaluable when you have to modify a door opening or cut into a wall for a new door.

STUD WALL CONSTRUCTION

Stud walls make up the basic framework of a house. A stud wall's components include the sole plate or bottom plate, the vertical studs, and two members across the top—the top plate and cap plate, sometimes together called a double top plate. Stud walls are usually built from 2×4 lumber, although some houses have 2×6 walls. Framing is nailed together with 16-penny (16d) nails.

Studs are generally laid out on 16-inch centers, but 24-inch centers are not uncommon. This spacing ensures that the edges of standard 4-foot-wide sheets of plywood, wallboard, and other building materials will fall on a stud.

A framing member called a header (shown below) spans a door opening, where there are no studs to carry the load of the floor or roof above. Headers are often built of 2× stock.

The header fits between two full-length king studs. Shorter trimmer studs are nailed to those studs to support each end of the header.

Building codes may require double trimmer studs for an opening wider than 5 or 6 feet or when the header carries an exceptional load. Special requirements may apply where earthquakes are likely.

WALLS OFTEN HIDE SURPRISES

You may run into wires, pipes, heating ducts, or other hardware while altering a wall.

Framing in houses built to resist earthquakes or wind may incorporate framing anchors—metal braces that provide more strength than nails alone—or hold-downs, which look like threaded pipe running vertically through the wall or attached to a stud. Don't disturb any of this hardware without consulting an engineer—it's an integral part of the home's design to withstand earthquakes or storms.

You may also run across electrical, telephone, or cable TV wires, heating ducts, and plumbing. Find out more about dealing with these on pages 15–17.

FRAMING HINTS: HEADERS

Headers must be adequate for the load they carry. The table below is a guide for sizing headers in a one-story house. Always check local building codes or consult an engineer before modifying your walls.

Opening width	Header size
Up to 4 feet	2×4
4 to 6 feet	2×6
6 to 8 feet	2×8
8 to 10 feet	2×10
10 to 12 feet	2×12

To build a header for a 2×4 wall, sandwich a piece of ⅜-inch plywood between two pieces of lumber of the appropriate size for your opening. Glue and screw or nail the

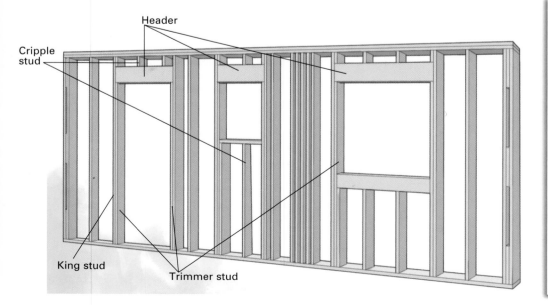

Header

Cripple stud

King stud

Trimmer stud

LUMBER GRADES

The wood-products industry grades lumber for different uses. Residential framing calls for lumber marked at least as Standard, Stud, or No. 2 grade, unless local building codes demand otherwise. When altering framing, use lumber of the same grades; lesser grades may not be strong enough.

pieces together. For 2×6 walls, you'll need to stack up three pieces of lumber and two layers of plywood for the correct thickness.

Install short, or cripple, studs in the space between the top of the header and the bottom of the double top plate, following the wall's stud spacing. If the space is so short that studs would split, simply use a wider header. You can shim the top or bottom of the header with lumber or plywood strips to eliminate the gap.

In a wall laid out with 24-inch stud centers, place your short studs directly beneath joists or rafters that rest on the double top. With 16-inch centers, this isn't as crucial.

SAFETY

Don't attempt any jobs without appropriate safety equipment. Always put on safety glasses or goggles, even if you wear glasses. Wear long sleeves, long pants, and sturdy shoes. A hard hat increases safety on many home jobs.

And don't forget about dust hazards that accompany building and demolition. Wear a lightweight paper mask to filter the dust; an approved respirator if you're disturbing old lead paint. A glance at the mask will show how much dust would have gotten into your lungs.

Construction noise can permanently damage your hearing, so protect yourself with earplugs, at least. Foam ones are readily available, cheap, and effective. Or you can don the larger hearing protectors that cover your ears and look like a flying ace's headphones.

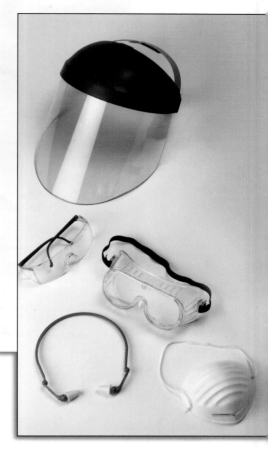

FRAMING HINTS: USE AN EXISTING STUD

You can save time, effort, and lumber by locating a new wall opening so an existing stud serves as one side, as shown in the drawing below. This may not be precisely where you wanted the opening, and if you're just putting in one door, the labor and expense may not be a factor. But in multiple installations, it might prove to be worthwhile when considering time and cost.

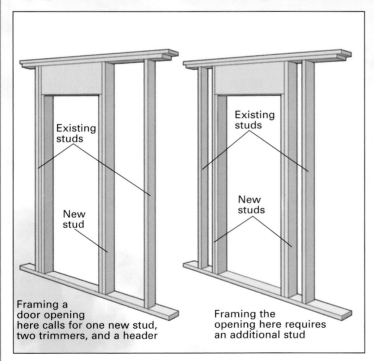

Existing studs

New stud

Framing a door opening here calls for one new stud, two trimmers, and a header

Existing studs

New studs

Framing the opening here requires an additional stud

PERMITS AND CODES

While you probably won't need a building permit to replace old doors in existing openings, most jurisdictions require one for new door openings. Check with your local building inspector to find out what's required.

Building codes are designed to prevent unsafe or hazardous construction in homes. Local codes stem from three recognized national codes: the Basic National Building Code, the Standard Building Code, and the Uniform Building Code. These model codes establish criteria for all aspects of construction, but local codes may go beyond their requirements when conditions dictate.

Securing a permit can save you problems later when you want to sell the house. With a permit, a building inspector will check out the work and ensure that you're not creating hazards or structural weaknesses in your home. A potential buyer doesn't get such assurances for work done without a permit or inspection.

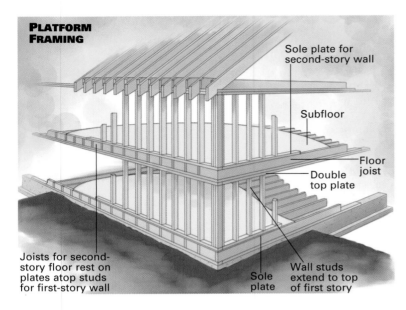

PLATFORM FRAMING

Sole plate for second-story wall

Subfloor

Floor joist

Double top plate

Joists for second-story floor rest on plates atop studs for first-story wall

Sole plate

Wall studs extend to top of first story

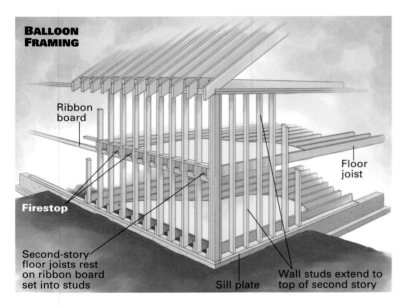

BALLOON FRAMING

Ribbon board

Floor joist

Firestop

Second-story floor joists rest on ribbon board set into studs

Sill plate

Wall studs extend to top of second story

FIRESTOPS

In balloon framing, you will encounter firestops, which are usually 2×4 blocks between studs. These prevent fire from spreading upward through the cavities in the wall. (In platform framing, the wall plates accomplish the same thing.) Firestops, made of either noncombustible or other approved material, are usually found in these locations:

■ Walls, partitions, and furred spaces at ceiling and floor levels;
■ Between stair framing members at the top and bottom;
■ Around chimneys, fireplaces, vents, pipes, at ceiling and floor levels with noncombustible material;
■ Between floor joists at the sill and girder.

Local building codes may require firestops in other locations. Replace firestops when you remove a wall.

OPENING A WALL

LOAD-BEARING WALLS

Before you cut into any wall, determine whether it is a load-bearing wall, one that carries weight from above, such as a floor, ceiling, or roof. A nonbearing wall acts as a partition and supports only its own weight.

■ Bearing walls generally run perpendicular to the floor, ceiling, or roof framing, which rests on the top plate of the bearing wall. You can usually see the direction of the framing in the attic, basement, or crawl space.

Seeing which way the floor joists run in the second floor of a house can be more difficult. Normally they run in the same direction as the first floor and ceiling. To be certain, scan the floor with an inexpensive electronic stud finder to look for joists.

Locate at least three or four consecutive joists to make sure you aren't just hitting some miscellaneous blocking. And be aware that framing sometimes changes direction.

■ A gable-end wall of a house is a special case. It does not generally stand perpendicular to the floor and roof framing and may carry considerable weight of its own, particularly if it is large and has a heavy finish, such as stucco. Posts in the gable-end walls may support a roof ridge beam. The beam's load must be supported if you make openings in the gable-end wall below it.

■ If the wall you need to cut into is a bearing wall, set up temporary supports for the ceiling, floor, or roof that it supports. How you go about that depends on whether the house is built with platform or balloon framing, as explained below.

PLATFORM FRAMING VS. BALLOON FRAMING

Platform framing—sometimes known as western framing—is a common method for house construction. In theory and practice, it's simple—walls are built on top of a platform: the floor. For other floor levels, the platform is built on top of the lower walls.

While most new houses are platform-framed, you'll find older homes and some new ones built with balloon framing. Some builders prefer balloon framing for two-story houses with stone or brick veneer siding.

In balloon framing, the wall studs and first-floor joists rest on a sill, and the studs run up to the full height of the wall without interruption (see illustration at left). Joists for higher floors rest on a 1×4 ribbon board cut into the studs and set flush with their inside edges. The floor joists are nailed to the sides of the studs.

TEMPORARY SUPPORTS IN PLATFORM FRAMING

To support a ceiling or floor above the wall in which you plan to cut an opening, construct a temporary stud wall 3 to 4 feet back from the existing wall. This will support the joists and still leave space for you to work.

Build the temporary wall much like a permanent wall, with studs spaced on 16-inch centers, a bottom plate, and a top plate. Build the wall flat on the floor, just short enough not to touch the ceiling. Tip it into place, plumb it with a level, and tack the bottom plate to the floor with double-headed nails. Then drive shims in from each side of the top plate at each floor joist location. Rather than using door-jamb shims, pick up a bundle of No.1 side-wall shingles. They won't be crushed under a load.

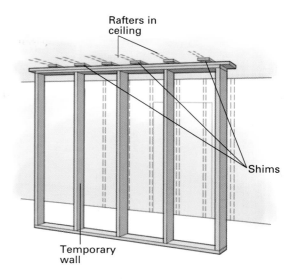

Before cutting into a wall in a platform-framed house, build a temporary stud wall to support the ceiling rafters behind the area where you'll make the new opening.

Rafters in ceiling

Shims

Temporary wall

TEMPORARY SUPPORTS FOR BALLOON FRAMING

A balloon-framed home calls for a different approach. Shoring is still necessary, but because the overhead load in balloon framing comes all the way down the wall, you must support the wall studs themselves rather than the ceiling above. Do this with a waler, a temporary horizontal cleat, attached to the wall.

Prepare the wall for the waler by removing the covering, as described on pages 16 and 17. Then tack a 2×8 waler across the top of the studs. Drill holes through the waler into each stud and attach it with $\frac{3}{8}$-inch lag screws 5 inches long. For extra support, cut a 2×4 brace to fit under each end of the waler. You can now safely cut studs below the waler to frame the opening.

Lag-screw a waler [A] to the wall studs above the proposed opening in a balloon-framed structure. Support the waler at each end with studs [B] running to the floor.

Studs to be cut for new door opening

PLUMBING IN THE WALLS

You may find water, gas, or DWV (drain, waste, and vent) lines in the wall you want to cut through.

Water pipes will be galvanized steel, copper, or plastic; gas lines, plain steel pipe (black pipe). DWV lines will be cast iron or plastic pipes, ranging in size from 1½ inches to 4 inches in diameter.

With basic plumbing skills, you can reroute copper or plastic water pipes yourself (see *Ortho's All About Plumbing Basics*), but galvanized-steel lines should be left to a plumber. Do not attempt any work on gas lines yourself; call a plumber.

Bring in the plumber, too, for necessary work on DWV lines. Modification of this system requires an understanding of drainage and venting principles governed by plumbing codes. Water flows through these pipes only by gravity, so you can't get away with sending a pipe on a detour over the top of the opening. (In some instances, you'll have to move the planned opening rather than reroute the DWV lines.) A plumber can tell you how to alter a plastic DWV system yourself, but modifying cast iron piping requires specialized equipment and should be left to the professional.

Install steel protector plates on the edge of framing members where a wire or pipe passes through. This will prevent you from driving a wallboard nail or a trim nail into the wire or pipe later.

PREPARING FOR THE CUT

NEW OPENING IN PLATFORM FRAMING

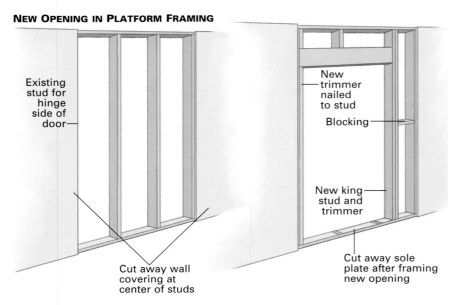

Existing stud for hinge side of door

New trimmer nailed to stud

Blocking

New king stud and trimmer

Cut away wall covering at center of studs

Cut away sole plate after framing new opening

For an exterior wall, remove the interior wall covering and complete the framing modifications before you cut the new opening through the exterior wall covering. This protects the work area from the elements as long as possible. Work from one side of an interior wall, too, to confine the mess.

If there's insulation in the wall, wear a dust mask, long pants, and a long sleeve shirt while you remove it. Shut off the electricity to any fixtures on the wall, including switches that control fixtures elsewhere. You can run extension cords for lights and tools from other outlets on a different circuit.

GETTING INTO THE WALL

■ Remove any trim from the wall. Remove cover plates from outlets and switches and take down any wall-mounted fixtures.
■ Remove the wallboard. In a small room, it may be easier to uncover the entire wall. To remove wallboard from the whole wall, cut through the taped joint in the corners of the room and along the ceiling with a utility knife. Cut completely through the joint so you won't peel the face paper off the adjacent wallboard. Then, pry off the wallboard or cut it into pieces.

To remove wallboard from a section of the wall, mark vertical lines from floor to ceiling 1 or 2 feet to the left and right of the new opening. Locate the next stud past each mark. Draw a cutting line down the center of each of these studs. Cutting to the center of a stud on each side of the opening provides a nailing surface for the new wall covering later.
■ Cut along the taped joint at the ceiling with a utility knife. Then cut through the wallboard to the stud along each cutting line. You can make this cut with a utility knife, but it's a time-consuming job because you'll keep running into nail heads.

Instead, fit your circular saw with a flooring blade or another type suitable for cutting into nails. Adjust the saw's cutting depth to be slightly deeper than the thickness of the wallboard—say $9/16$ or $5/8$ inch for $1/2$-inch board. Then saw along the line. Finish the cuts near the floor with a utility knife or handsaw. This method is fast and leaves a relatively straight edge, but it raises a lot of dust. Wear safety glasses, a dust mask, and hearing protection.
■ After you've cut the wallboard top and edges loose, pull the wallboard off the studs. You may have to punch a hole in it to get a grip—watch out for wire or pipes behind the wall when punching through. Once you do have a starting place, you can pull the board out in chunks and pry it loose with a flat steel prybar.
■ Remove the studs where the new opening will be. To do this, cut them in half with a circular saw, reciprocating saw, or handsaw. Then pull the ends toward you and wrest them free.

FRAMING THE NEW OPENING

■ Install the first king stud. If an existing stud will serve as one of the king studs, check it for plumb. If it isn't plumb and you can't adjust it easily, nail the new king stud to it, shimming as needed.

To install a new king stud, mark its location on the wall's top plate. Using a plumb bob, transfer the mark to the bottom plate. Cut the stud to length.

Then cut the trimmer stud to length for the same side of the opening. (Trimmer stud length equals the height of the rough opening required, minus $1\frac{1}{2}$ inches to allow for the

HEATING PIPES AND DUCTS

If your home is heated by hot water flowing through radiators or baseboard convectors, pipes for the system may run through the walls. When pipes or other parts of the heating system must be moved, call a heating contractor to do it. How the pipes run can drastically affect the performance of the system.

With forced-air heating, you may find ductwork in the walls. You may be able to move these yourself if you have a crawl space or basement and the parts are readily available. You'll probably need to hire a heating contractor if special parts must be fabricated.

NEW OPENING IN BALLOON FRAMING

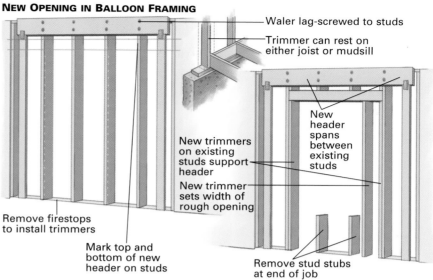

Waler lag-screwed to studs

Trimmer can rest on either joist or mudsill

New trimmers on existing studs support header

New header spans between existing studs

New trimmer sets width of rough opening

Remove firestops to install trimmers

Mark top and bottom of new header on studs

Remove stud stubs at end of job

thickness of the wall plate it sits on.) The rough opening for a door is usually 2 inches more than the door's height. (Check the manufacturer's specifications for the rough-opening height for a prehung door unit.) Nail the trimmer stud to the king stud, keeping the ends flush at the bottom.

Install the assembled king stud and trimmer stud. Align the king stud with the location marks, check for plumb, and attach the assembly to the top and bottom plates.

If the width of the studs already in the wall differs from the width of the studs you are installing, line up the outside face of the new studs flush with the outside face of the old studs. Then rip furring strips of the correct thickness to bring the inside face of the new studs in line with the existing framing.
■ With one king and one trimmer stud installed, lay out the width of the rough opening on the base plate. Measure the required distance from the face of the trimmer stud just installed, then draw a mark 1½ inches past that point to indicate the location of the second king stud. Transfer the mark to the top plate.
■ Cut and install the second king and trimmer studs, checking for plumb before you nail or screw them in.
■ Measure from king stud to king stud at the top of the trimmer studs to determine the header length. Assemble the header from 2× lumber and ⅜-inch plywood to give it the correct thickness (see page 12). Nail or screw the header in place. Complete the framing by cutting and installing the cripple studs between the header and top plate, spacing them to match the existing studs.
■ Once the new framing is in place, cut through the covering on the other side of the wall. This is easier if you first nail the wall covering to the framing around the new opening. Make the cut with a circular saw or a reciprocating saw. Finally, remove the bottom plate inside the opening. Saw the ends flush to the trimmer studs, using a handsaw or reciprocating saw. Then pry the plate from the floor.

ALTERING AN EXISTING OPENING

You can adapt the procedures above to change the size of an existing door opening. If the new opening will be smaller, install

new trimmer studs in one or both sides of the opening. Space them out from the old trimmers with blocking of 2× lumber. If the new opening will be larger than the existing one, add a new king stud and trimmer and replace the header.

WIRES IN THE WALLS

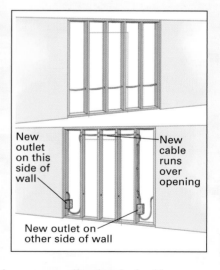

New outlet on this side of wall

New cable runs over opening

New outlet on other side of wall

You're likely to encounter wiring where you make an opening in the wall. You may find knob and tube wiring in older homes, identifiable by the porcelain insulators that attach the wiring to the framing. You might also run into metal conduit or flexible armored cable. Call an electrician for work with these installations unless you have experience with them.

Newer house wiring employs nonmetallic sheathed cable, which combines two insulated conductors and usually a ground conductor in a thermoplastic sheathing. Most do-it-yourselfers can alter this kind of wiring.

You can usually reroute wire around a planned door opening by installing a new outlet on either side of the opening. The two outlets can then be connected by a cable running over the top of the door opening or through the basement or crawlspace through holes in the floor. (Consult *Ortho's All About Wiring Basics* for more wiring information.)

WEATHERPROOFING

FLASHING AND FLASHING PAPER

Sheet-metal flashings and flashing paper are commonly used to keep water out of the joints in a building. Some builders prefer to use 15- or 30-pound felt paper, also called building felt, instead of flashing paper. A Z-flashing, a piece of sheet metal with the edges bent to opposite-facing right angles, is a common form of metal flashing for door openings. Metal flashing can be left exposed to weather, but flashing paper or felt must be covered for protection.

Flashing paper or felt paper have formed the traditional final line of defense in weatherproofing a wall. On a plain wall with no openings, these materials are installed horizontally, typically in courses 3 feet wide, starting at the bottom of the wall. Each higher course overlaps the one below it, like fish scales. Under the siding of newer homes, you'll find a white, paper-like membrane

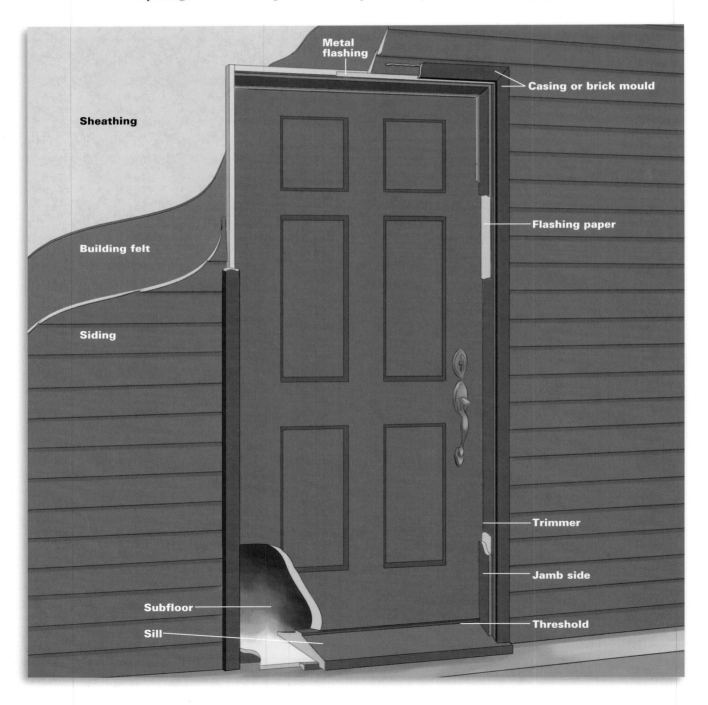

instead of felt or flashing paper. This is a housewrap, spun from synthetic fibers. It's usually wide enough to cover the wall without any seams.

Water that might find its way through a gap in the siding will not be able to pass through the paper or housewrap. This is pretty simple; the hard part is maintaining the water barrier around a door opening.

■ For a good start at weatherproofing the opening, tack strips of flashing paper or 15-pound felt paper around the rough opening before you install the door unit or jambs. You can use staples or roofing nails. First, install a strip across the bottom of the door opening. The bottom strip should overlap the existing paper below it.

Then run a strip along each side, overlapping the bottom strip. These side strips should slide under the paper that is above the opening.

■ On a door unit with a nailing fin, the fin acts like a flashing for the head of the door. The paper above the door should overlap the fin so that water cannot get under the fin. Cutting the wide felt paper that's already on the house to fit over the top nailing fin can be difficult. It's easier to cut a narrow strip of felt paper or a length of flashing paper long enough to overlap the side flashing paper. Then notch the felt paper on the house to clear the fin, and slip the new strip up under it. If using housewrap, the top fin slips under the wrap and the side and bottom fins go over it. This may take a little cutting at the top corners of the housewrap. Seal the cuts in the wrap with caulk.

Exterior trim will cover the fin. If the wall will be covered with stucco, shingles, or siding, you could add a metal Z-flashing over the head, slipping it under the weatherproofing paper or housewrap, too.

■ When using plywood or hardboard sheet siding, a door with a fin is best installed first. You can then cut the siding to fit around the door and cover the fin. Caulk the gaps, and install wood trim to cover the joint between the door and the plywood. Some plywood siding is rated for use without underlying paper, so you may find none under existing plywood siding.

■ Sometimes you may want to install a door with nail-on wood trim right over existing siding. In this case, hiding the flashings could be difficult. You could install a door over the siding with no felt or flashing, then caulk around the trim, but that's not recommended. For truly trouble-free weatherproofing, you'll need a Z-flashing. One solution is to fabricate a Z-flashing with a small return that tucks

into a shallow groove in the siding, which can then be caulked. The groove can be made very easily with a circular saw. Set the blade at an appropriate depth and tack a straight piece of wood across the door trim to serve as a guide. Finish the ends with a chisel.

CAULKING MATERIALS

There are plenty of caulking materials to choose from today. Here are some of them:

■ **POLYURETHANE** caulks are some of the toughest and most reliable caulks, designed for commercial applications. Use polyurethane where the bead will be exposed to sun and weather.

■ **SILICONE** is often touted as being indestructible. The caulk may be, but it has a tendency to let go of porous materials such as wood. It does adhere tenaciously to glass, metal, and tile, so it's frequently used in bathrooms. But for exposed beads, such as around trim, polyurethane is far superior.

■ **BUTYL CAULK** is an old reliable formulation that is available everywhere. Butyl has adequate durability, particularly if it will be covered by trim. It also sticks well. It is stringy and messy to work with, however.

■ **LATEX AND ACRYLIC LATEX CAULKS** and acrylic latex caulk with silicone added are all widely available household caulks. These aren't durable enough for harsh exposures, although they can work well where sheltered or indoors.

WEATHER STRIPPING

To keep the drafts at bay, you'll need weather stripping. Prehung exterior door units ordinarily come with weather stripping already installed. For other door installations, you'll have to add weather stripping.

Various styles of weather stripping are sold at home improvement centers and lumberyards, ranging from foam tape to aluminum moldings with vinyl gaskets. Regional preferences and the local climate usually determine the kinds of weather stripping available in your area. Some types require additional clearance around the door. If you're hanging your own door, decide on the weather stripping you want to use first, so you can accommodate it right from the start

Door sweeps and door bottoms seal out drafts at the bottom of the door. The best ones are adjustable so they can seal snugly while allowing the door to operate smoothly. Some sweeps are spring-loaded so they lift slightly when the door is open, providing more clearance when opening over thick rugs.

INSTALLING A PREHUNG EXTERIOR DOOR

This section lists the general steps to install a prehung entry door in a rough opening. If you are replacing an existing exterior door with a prehung entry door, you'll need to remove the old jambs and sill from the opening, along with any interior and exterior trim. Prehung entry doors come with or without trim.

Unpack the door and make sure that it swings the right way. Removing the door would lighten the unit and make it easier to handle, but you'll usually be better off if you leave it in place with the blocks and retainers installed at the factory. This will keep the unit square so you can avoid problems later. Enlist a helper to assist with the job.

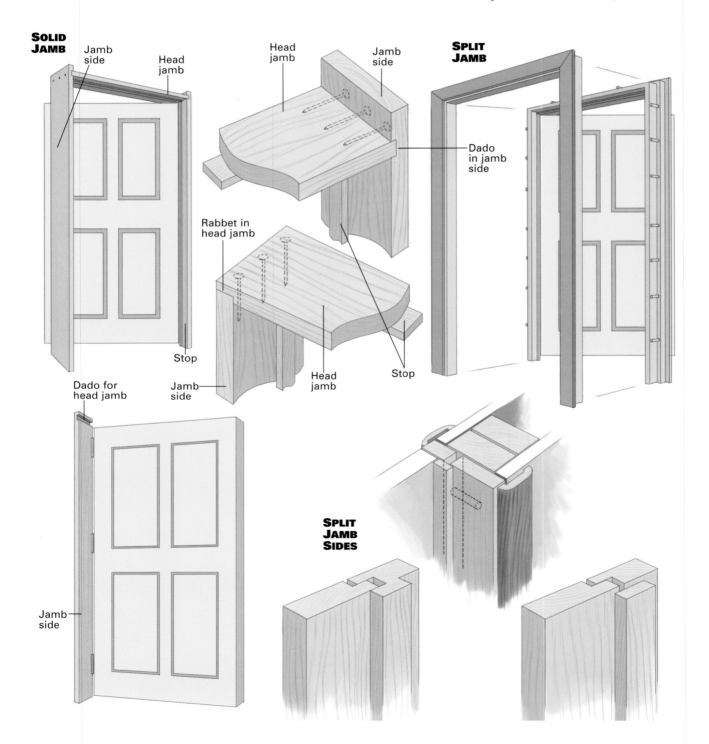

SOLID JAMB

Jamb side

Head jamb

Head jamb

Jamb side

SPLIT JAMB

Dado in jamb side

Rabbet in head jamb

Stop

Jamb side

Head jamb

Stop

Dado for head jamb

Jamb side

Jamb side

SPLIT JAMB SIDES

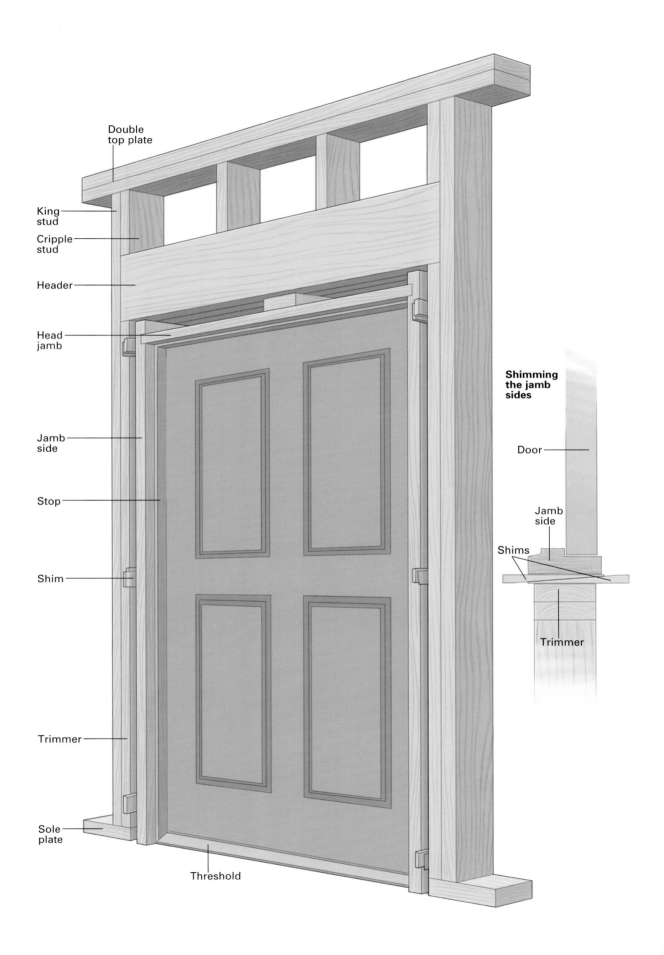

Double top plate

King stud

Cripple stud

Header

Head jamb

Jamb side

Stop

Shim

Trimmer

Sole plate

Threshold

Shimming the jamb sides

Door

Jamb side

Shims

Trimmer

INSTALLING A PREHUNG EXTERIOR DOOR
continued

■ Slide the door unit into the opening to test its fit. Shim the frame to plumb and level it. Inspect the gap between the door and jamb all around. If the door is perfectly square, the space should be even all the way around. If there isn't enough space in one spot, that's where the door will bind.

■ If the unit has brick molding attached, trace the outline of the molding on the house siding. Remove the door and frame from the opening.

■ Saw along the line to cut away the siding down to the sheathing. You can make the cut with a circular saw with a blade that won't be damaged by nails. Set the saw's cutting depth slightly deeper than the thickness of the siding. Complete the corners and square them up with a chisel.

■ Slip an 8-inch-wide strip of building paper between the siding and sheathing along the top and sides of the rough opening. Install a drip cap at the top.

■ Lay a bead of caulk along the subfloor and the building paper edges.

■ Place the door unit into the opening again. Center it, and slip pairs of shims between the jamb and framing from the inside. Space the shims 12 inches apart and at the hinge and lockset locations.

■ Plumb the door jamb, checking it with a level. Adjust the shims to hold the unit plumb and level. Fill spaces between the jamb with insulation. You can spray in an expanding foam or stuff fiberglass insulation into the gap.

■ As a rule, the jambs are shimmed, then nailed to the framing with 10d casing or finish nails through the shims into the framing. Designs differ, however, so follow the manufacturer's instructions. The sill is usually screwed to the floor. Don't drive the nails in all the way yet. Test the door for binding, and adjust the shims as needed. Then set the nails, and trim the ends off the shims.

■ For security, anchor the hinges to the house framing with long screws. Install the lockset and strike plate.

■ Adjust the threshold, following the manufacturer's instructions.

■ Nail the brick molding on the outside, and caulk between it and the siding. Attach the trim with hot-dipped galvanized nails. Countersink the nails, then fill the holes with putty, sand smooth, and paint the trim. If the door is already painted and you don't want to fill nail holes, use stainless-steel ring-shank finishing nails available at many lumberyards. They're expensive but it only takes a few to install a door. They will not rust and cause streaks, so you don't need to countersink them. The heads are fairly small, too.

■ Install the interior trim. Countersink the nails, fill all nail holes, and paint the trim. Apply weather stripping as required.

MATCHING THE SILL TO THE FLOOR

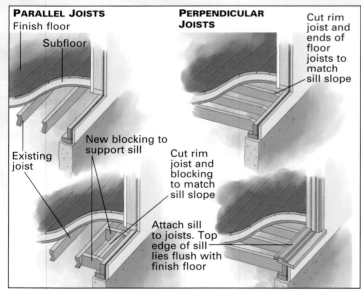

When installing a prehung entry door unit, you may have to cut away some of the flooring or subflooring to place the doorsill at the correct height. This height will vary depending on the door and on the finish floor. A wood sill usually sits so the back edge lies flush with the finish floor. The joint is then covered with another piece—the threshold. How the floor will be cut away depends on the construction of the house. The important thing is that the joint between the sill and the floor must be fully supported. You may need to add blocking to accomplish this.

MAKE SURE YOUR FLOOR IS LEVEL

If the gaps at the top and bottom of the door are not even all the way across when you set the unit in the opening, the subfloor may not be level under the door. Try correcting the condition with shims. If that doesn't work, the floor itself may need repair. This can be complicated and expensive, so seek expert advice if you have a crooked floor.

VINTAGE HARDWARE FOR NEW DOORS

Whether you're restoring an older home or embellishing a new one, the elegant look of brass or copper vintage door knobs, back plates, and hinges has become more popular in recent years. But installing antique hardware on doors they were not originally part of can be time-consuming and exasperating. On the plus side, most locksets made over a hundred years ago were well-built, so if you have them and can install them, they'll probably continue to do the job. If parts are missing, however, finding replacements can be difficult. If the cylinders are broken, the problem is worse.

Fortunately, there has been a great increase in availability of new hardware that looks exactly like many of the vintage designs. While not inexpensive, these solid brass, copper, or flat-iron replications look authentic, but are much easier to install and maintain.

Cleaning existing hardware often involves little more than stripping off layers of paint that may have actually protected the hardware from damage for decades. Use household ammonia and plenty of time. Extended soaking lifts off the crusty layers. Some gentle wire brushing with a very fine bronze or steel brush or a handheld rotary tool works fine for cleaning all the crevices, even in old lock mechanisms.

Except for some cleaning or oiling, door locks that still operate should generally be left alone. You should take locks that need extensive service or repairs to a locksmith.

If your heart is set on antique locks and back plates for new doors, be sure to get doors that haven't been predrilled with holes for modern hardware. Modern doors use locks that fit into round holes bored through the door. Locks for old doors usually fit into deep mortises cut into the door edge, with smaller holes through the faces of the door. The back plates and rosettes that go with these aren't big enough to cover the holes in standard doors, so you'll have to custom-make your own holes in doors.

You probably won't have a ready-made pattern for installing old mortise locks. Having the door that originally held the hardware helps by providing a pattern for a new door. You can make cardboard templates for mortise sizes, shaft locations, and the like.

When shopping for vintage or reproduction hardware, consider these suggestions:
- Buy complete items with no missing parts, especially latches, locks, and mechanical doorbells. Avoid buying locks that need repair.
- Comparison shop—today's numerous options make it a buyer's market for reproductions.
- Don't overclean flea market finds with stiff wire brushes or caustic solutions. Clean them with the mildest paint removers or ammonia. Consider leaving unpainted metal's natural patina. Bronze, brass, and other metals typically mellow into various shades of red, rose, verdigris, and gold.
- Be wary of overly shiny hardware being sold as antique, even if it's heavy and seems old. It may be a reproduction. If it's the real thing, excessive polishing and buffing can damage original small details.
- Test brass items with a magnet. If the magnet sticks, the item isn't solid brass; it's steel with brass plating.
- Examine custom orders carefully for signs of bad workmanship or attempts to cover it up.

INSTALLING A SLIDING PATIO DOOR

Sliding patio doors made of metal, fiberglass, and plastic are installed in much the same way as prehung doors. Most feature a nailing fin, which runs around the top and sides of the jamb on the outside.
■ Nail the fin to the sheathing on the outside of the house; siding or trim will cover it. Jambs and sills are also usually attached to the house framing by screws. Metal- and vinyl-clad door frames most closely resemble

metal-framed doors. The cladding itself may include a nailing fin. Sometimes a nailing fin is provided to attach to the unit on site.
■ Have the door unit on hand at the time you do the rough framing. If this isn't possible, be sure you have a copy of the installation instructions or manufacturer's rough-opening specifications so you can make the rough opening the correct size.

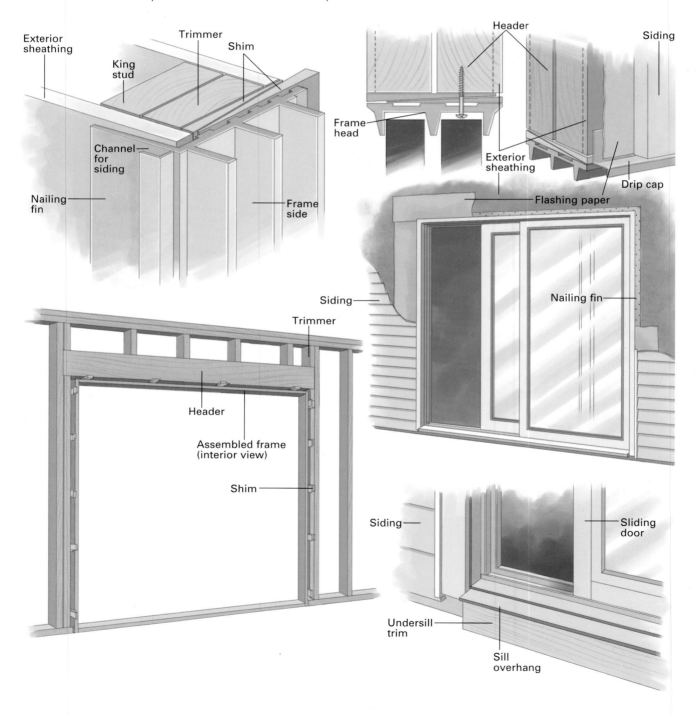

DOOR JAMBS

Although prehung door units are common today, you can still assemble a jamb yourself, install it, and hang a door in it. You may have to do this if you can't find a prehung unit that meets your needs. The procedures are similar for interior or exterior doors, but the jambs will differ somewhat.

■ Exterior door jambs are commonly rabbeted, but flat ones are sometimes installed. The rabbeted sides and head of the rabbeted jamb create the door stop. With a flat jamb, separate stops are nailed on. Exterior jambs are installed with a sill at the bottom. The sill slopes slightly to the outside so water won't run into the house. A threshold on top of the sill seals against the bottom of the door and covers the joint between the sill and the finished floor inside.

■ Interior jambs are flat and are often made of thinner, finger-jointed material. Interior doors don't require a sill or threshold, although a thin saddle or metal molding may be installed in the opening to bridge different types of floor covering.

■ To hang your own door, you'll need the door itself, a jamb set, a sill for an exterior door, three butt hinges, a threshold, a lockset, doorstops (if not furnished with the jamb set), exterior and interior trim, and weather stripping.

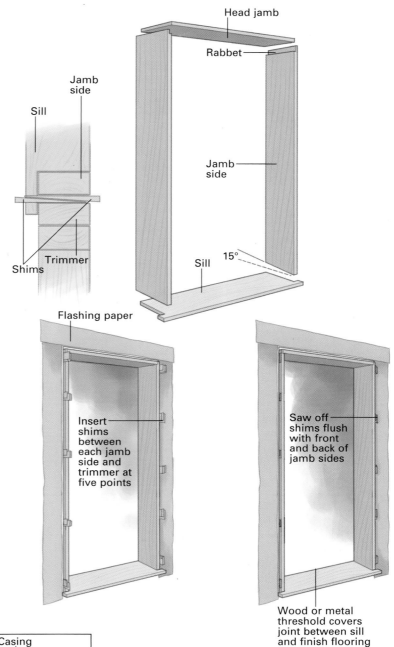

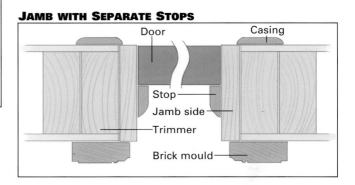

RABBETED JAMB

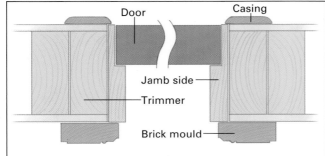

JAMB WITH SEPARATE STOPS

BUILDING A JAMB

■ Buy a jamb set, which includes two jamb sides and the head (top). You can buy jamb sets at lumberyards and home improvement centers. You'll need to specify the door width and height as well as the thickness of your wall. Jambs are available for a number of standard wall thicknesses; if none of them match your wall, you can rip overwidth jamb parts to size or build up the edges of a narrower jamb.

■ For an exterior door, buy a sill along with the jamb. Sills are made of hardwood and should have a groove on the underside near the front to prevent water from creeping along the bottom to the house. If it doesn't have one, cut a ¼-inch-deep circular-saw kerf about 1 inch from the front edge.

■ It's easier to form the hinge mortises in the jamb side before you assemble and install the jamb. See Installing Hinges (next page) for information about locating hinges. Cut the hinge mortises as shown on page 27.

■ Measure the jamb head to ensure that the jamb will be the right width for your door. The jamb opening should be ¼ inch wider than the width of the door. Fit the head into the rabbets at the top of the jamb sides, and nail the sides to the head with 8d casing nails.

■ Measure the distance between the jamb sides at the top. Then cut the sill to length to give the same width at the bottom. Slide the sill into place and drill pilot holes through the jamb sides into the sill. Screw or nail the jamb sides to the sill. Square the assembly by measuring from corner to corner diagonally. When both diagonal measurements are the same, the assembly is square. Tack diagonal braces across two corners of the jamb to keep it square.

Because an interior jamb won't have a sill, temporarily tack a piece of 1×2 across the jamb sides at the bottom to brace them.

INSTALLING THE JAMB

■ The sill of an exterior jamb should sit flush with the finished floor. In new construction where the finished flooring is not yet installed, set the jambs and sill to allow for the additional floor layers.

In some cases, you may have to trim the floor joists under the sill with a saw or chisel to set the sill at the correct level. And you must support the back edge of the sill and the edge of the flooring where it meets the sill.

To provide support when the joists run parallel to the sill, nail blocks of the same dimension as the joists between the joists on either side of the door opening. Cut two support joists to length and nail them through the blocks, as illustrated on page 22. One will support the flooring, and the other will hold the inner edge of the sill.

■ Slide the jamb into the rough opening. Slip shims between the jamb sides and the framing, placing them every 12 inches along the sides and behind each hinge location.

■ Ensure that the frame is plumb and square. Check the head jamb with a level. Then tack the hinge-side jamb to the trimmer at the top and bottom.

■ On an interior jamb, remove the temporary brace and adjust the width of the jambs at the bottom to match the width at the top. Tack the other side of the jamb to the framing. Check again that the jamb is square by placing a steel framing square in the corners. Check that the head jamb and sill (for an exterior jamb) are level.

When everything is square, nail the jambs to the trimmer studs with casing nails through the shims. Fasten the sill to the framing.

FITTING THE DOOR

■ Measure the door opening, and cut or plane the door width to ¼ inch less than the width of the jamb opening. Allow additional space around the door for weather stripping, if necessary. If the door is already bored or mortised for the lockset, trim the hinge side.

■ Allow ⅛ inch of clearance at the top and bottom. You can measure and trim the bottom of the door to clear the threshold and finished flooring later.

■ Bevel the inner edge of the lock stile ⅛ inch with a jack plane. This prevents the door edge from catching on the jamb or weather stripping as it swings.

SUGGESTED DOOR HINGE SIZES

Door Thickness (inches)	Door Width (inches)	Hinge Size (inches)
¾–1⅛ (cabinets)	Up to 24	2½
⅞–1⅛ (screen, storm)	Up to 36	3
1⅜	Up to 32	3½
	36	4
1¾	Up to 36	4½
	37–42	5
2 (heavy entry door)	Up to 42	5 or 6

CUTTING MORTISES

Hinge mortises can be cut with a router and a commercially available hinge mortise template, a hinge marker, or the tried-and-true hammer and chisel.

■ When using a router and template, carefully read the instructions that come with the template. You'll need a straight routing bit and a guide bushing for the router. The basic procedure is to clamp the template to the edge of the door, adjust the router bit to the depth of the hinge thickness, then rout the mortise.

Hardware stores, lumberyards, and home improvement centers sell hinges with rounded corners to fit routed mortises. If you have hinges with square corners, square the corners of the mortise with a chisel.

■ Cut the mortises by hand with a sharp ¾- or ½-inch chisel and a mallet. Start by marking the hinge's outline on the face of the jamb or edge of the door, using a sharp pencil or knife. Mark the depth on the adjacent edge of the jamb or face of the door. Next, establish the outline of the mortise with the chisel. Holding it vertically with the flat side of the blade against the guideline, drive the chisel in to the depth of the mortise. Do this all around the hinge outline.

Make a series of similar cuts about ¼ inch apart inside the mortise area. Stick a piece of masking tape on the back of the chisel to serve as a depth gauge.

Remove the waste wood in the mortise by driving the chisel from the edge toward the center of the mortise, with the back of the chisel on the depth line and the bevel facing up. Set the hinge in the mortise to check the fit. Make any final adjustments and clean up the corners.

INSTALLING HINGES

On exterior doors up to 7 feet tall, install three 4-inch butt hinges. On doors over 7 feet high, use four. Interior doors that are only 1⅜ inches thick normally hang on two 3½-inch hinges, although you can use three for an unusually heavy door. Hinges are mortised into the door edge.

■ Exact hinge locations vary according to taste, but one common practice is to place the top of the highest hinge 7 inches from the top of the door and the bottom of the lowest one 11 inches from the bottom. Additional hinges are spaced evenly between these. When you are preparing a door to hang in a jamb with mortises already cut, match the hinge locations on the door to those in the jamb. Position the door in the opening, leaving ⅛ inch clearance at the top. Transfer the hinge locations from the jamb to the door edge carefully and accurately.

■ Set the door on edge to cut the mortises, bracing it against a workbench or holding it with easy-to-make door bucks as shown on page 29. Trace the outline of the hinge on the edge with a sharp pencil or a knife. Allow the leaf to extend ¼ inch past the front the edge so that the knuckle will not bind against the casing when the door is fully open. Remember that the knuckle goes on the side of the opening the door swings toward—the inside of the house for exterior doors.

■ Cut or rout the mortises (see the box above). Lay the hinges in place, then centerpunch each screw hole. Drill pilot holes for the hinge screws, and attach the hinges. Be sure the holes are straight; crooked screws will move the hinge off center.

■ If the door jamb is not already mortised, stand the door in the jamb opening. Keeping the face of the door flush with the jamb, shim the door at the bottom so the top is ⅛ inch below the head jamb. Mark the hinge locations on the jamb with a sharp pencil or knife. This is easier said than done, so get someone to help you. Remove the door and trace hinge outlines onto the jamb where marked. Then cut the mortises in the jamb.

BUILDING A JAMB
continued

Stop

Wedge to hold door
in correct position

While you hold the door closed at the proper position, have a helper trace the outside edge of the door along the jamb with a sharp pencil. For an exterior door, allow space for the weather stripping you'll install, if necessary.

Measure and cut the stops to length, miter-cutting the corners. First, nail on the head stop along the line, then nail on the two legs.

INSTALL THE THRESHOLD

Remove the door again and install the threshold to cover the gap between the sill and the finish floor. For a hardwood threshold, drill pilot holes to prevent splitting the wood, and nail the threshold in place. Install an aluminum threshold with screws. Drill pilot holes in the sill for the screws. Remember that the threshold must fit snugly between the jamb sides.

You may need to trim the bottom of the door to fit over the threshold. To remove a small amount, plane the door.

Otherwise, cut the door with a circular saw equipped with a fine-toothed blade, such as is used for cutting plywood. With a portable circular saw, cut with the best side of the door facing down. To make a straight cut, clamp a straight-edged board to the door as a saw guide. Position it so the blade will cut slightly below the cutting line. Protect the door from the clamps with pieces of scrap wood. Lay masking tape over the cutting line on both sides of the door to minimize splintering. Make the cut, then plane the door to the cutting line.

Some aluminum thresholds with weather stripping require a beveled door bottom. Check the installation instructions if you installed this type of threshold. If a bevel is required, set the saw angle before you make the cut.

It works best to mark and cut the top hinge first. Put the door up, screw the top hinge to the jamb, and then check the other marks and make adjustments before you cut them.

If you attach the halves of a hinge separately and they don't line up when you put the door in place, loosen the screws on both leaves. While a helper supports the door, tap the leaves together. Insert the pin and tighten the screws.

When the door is up, check that it closes without binding anywhere. There should be a 1/8-inch gap along each side and across the top. For a smooth-swinging door, take it down and plane another 1/16 inch off the lock stile for 3/16 inch of clearance. Retain the bevel.

If the door sticks at the top of the jamb and the gap between door and jamb is wider at the bottom, the problem may be a jamb that is not plumb, a bottom-hinge mortise that is too deep, or a top-hinge mortise that is not deep enough.

To correct the first two problems, shim the bottom hinge. You can cut a shim from the cardboard box the hinges came in. Cut a strip the same height as the hinge, about 1/4 inch wide. Loosen the hinge on the jamb, slip the shim behind it, and retighten the screws.

If the door binds at the top because the top mortise wasn't cut deeply enough, remove the door and chisel the mortise deeper.

INSTALL THE STOPS

Install the stops in a flat jamb. You can buy stop moldings in several styles at lumberyards and home improvement centers.

FINISHING TOUCHES

Complete the installation by adding the trim (see page 30). Paint or stain the door. Apply a clear finish, such as polyurethane varnish, to stained or unpainted doors.

HOLDING DOORS FOR WORK

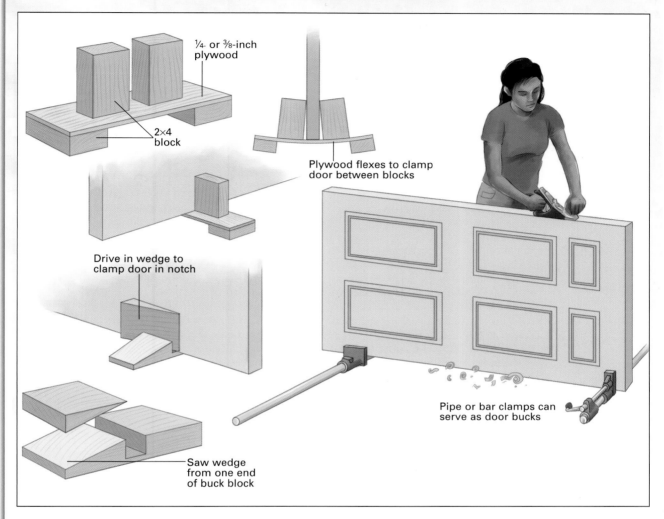

¼- or ⅜-inch plywood

2×4 block

Plywood flexes to clamp door between blocks

Drive in wedge to clamp door in notch

Saw wedge from one end of buck block

Pipe or bar clamps can serve as door bucks

One of the biggest challenges when working on a door is holding it steady. Here are some tips for holding doors.

When sawing a door shorter, lay it across a pair of sawhorses. Clamp it to the sawhorses for greater stability. You can make the cut with a portable circular saw or a handsaw.

To narrow a door by sawing a strip off the edge, rely again on sawhorses and clamps. To make the cut with a portable circular saw, clamp a guide to the door as shown on page 45.

To cut hinge mortises or plane an edge, it's easiest to work on a door that's standing on edge. You can hold a door on edge by pushing one end into a corner of a room at a 45-degree angle. You also can clamp the door to the legs of a table or workbench to hold it for work.

If you're going to be working on doors often, you need door bucks. Here are two easy-to-make door bucks and a way to use pipe or bar clamps you probably already own.

To use pipe or bar clamps as door bucks, just clamp them to an edge of the door, as shown in the illustration above. Face the clamps in opposite directions to give the door a steady footing. Place scraps of plywood or lumber between the jaw clamps and the door face for protection.

Make the bucks shown from scrap wood. For the plywood buck, cut two pieces of ¼- or ⅜-inch plywood 3½ inches wide and 12 inches long. Nail and glue two pieces of 2×4 about 4 inches long near the center of the plywood, as shown. Space

them apart by the thickness of your door, plus ⅛ inch.

Nail and glue two 2×4 legs to the bottom, as shown. To use the bucks, place the door in the slot between the 2×4s on top. The weight of the door will flex the plywood enough to clamp the door between the blocks.

Make the wedge door bucks from two 16-inch lengths of 2×4. Cut a 2¼-inch-wide notch 1 inch deep across the middle of each. Lay out the cutting line for the wedge on one end of each piece. Make the wedge about 1¼ inches thick at the end. Saw off the wedge-shaped piece.

To use the door bucks, set the door in the notches. Drive in the wedges to secure the door, as shown in the illustration.

TRIMMING OUT THE DOOR

Trim covers the gap between the door jamb and the siding. It also attaches the door unit to the house on some modern prehung entry doors. The trim also conveys a style, and it can be used to change the look of the door.

EXTERIOR TRIM

Many prehung entry door units come with the exterior trim already attached. For other exterior doors, you'll need to add the trim. Brick mold, generally available in two patterns, is the standard trim for an exterior door. But you can also trim the door opening with smooth or rough-sawn boards or other styles of moldings. You should try to match the look—if not the exact style—of other exterior trim on the house.

If you don't use standard moldings for painted exterior trim, select kiln-dried stock. (Stock moldings are usually kiln dried.) Otherwise you'll later find joints opening up from shrinkage, and the paint may fail as the trapped moisture tries to escape. (Many painters recommend priming and painting the back of the trim to give a more durable paint job.) For stained or clear-finished exterior trim, specify vertical-grain or quartersawn stock. It's more expensive than flat-grain lumber but will stand up to the elements better. Install exterior trim with stainless-steel nails to avoid rust streaking.

Finally, if you are going to paint the trim and the siding, be sure to caulk the joint between them well. If the trim is properly flashed and there is caulk under it, you can caulk the outside joints adequately with a siliconized acrylic caulk.

INTERIOR TRIM

The trim around an interior door opening is called casing. Several standard casing patterns are available at lumberyards and home improvement centers. The moldings are generally available in softwood, either finger-jointed or solid, and hardwoods, such as oak, birch, and mahogany. For trim that will be painted, the cheaper finger-jointed softwood moldings will suffice. If you'll be staining the moldings, use solid softwood or a hardwood. Some wood moldings are sold prefinished. You can also choose nonwood moldings, which are as easy to work as wood but resist splitting and warping.

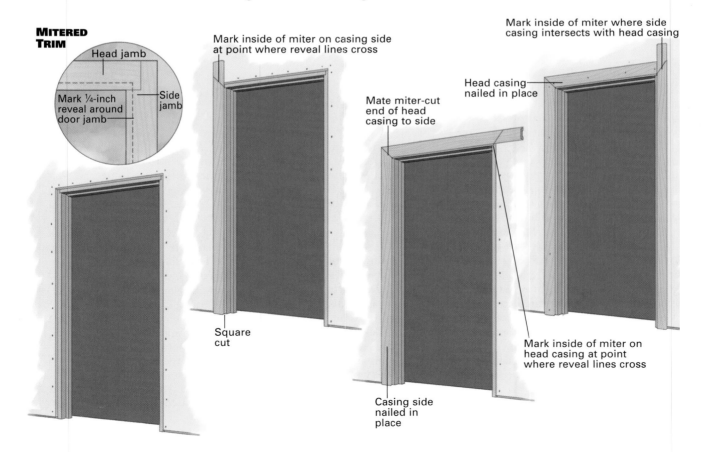

MITERED TRIM

Head jamb

Mark ¼-inch reveal around door jamb

Side jamb

Mark inside of miter on casing side at point where reveal lines cross

Square cut

Mate miter-cut end of head casing to side

Casing side nailed in place

Mark inside of miter where side casing intersects with head casing

Head casing nailed in place

Mark inside of miter on head casing at point where reveal lines cross

INSTALLING MITERED TRIM

Door trim is usually installed with mitered cuts at the corners. Ideally, the casing should be set back from the inner edges of the jamb by at least 3/16 inch, but no more than 1/4 inch. (This distance is called a reveal.) Here's how to install the trim:

■ Draw a guideline on the edge of the jamb sides and head to mark where the edge of the casing should be. To do this, adjust a combination square so that 3/16 inch protrudes, then slide the square along the jamb with a pencil tip following the end of the blade. Mark the head jamb in the same way,

■ Cut the bottom of the right side casing at a 90-degree angle. Place the casing on the side jamb, aligning it with the guideline. Mark the top of the casing where the guideline on the head jamb meets the edge of the casing. From that point, cut the casing upward at a 45-degree angle. Cut it precisely with a miterbox and backsaw or a power miter saw. Tack the side casing into place.

■ Miter-cut the right end of the head casing at 45 degrees and fit it to the side casing. Mark the left end at the point where the left-side guideline meets it. Miter-cut the left end, and tack up the head casing.

■ Cut the bottom end of the left side casing at a 90-degree angle and put it in place, overlapping the corner of the head molding. Mark where it meets the head casing, miter-cut it and tack it in place. If both corners look tight, drive the nails in, countersink them, and fill the holes.

Another method is to mark the reveal on the jamb edges, and cut and tack up the two side casings. Then, for the head casing, miter-cut both ends of a length of trim that extends 4 inches past the outer edges of each side casing. Fit the left end of the head casing against the left side casing, positioning it precisely on the guideline. Let the right end overlap the right side casing. Check the joint fit. A gap indicates that either the door jamb is out of square or your miter cuts aren't exactly 45 degrees. Check the joint on the other side in the same way. If one side fits, put it in place. Then, to compensate for the error, mark the top and bottom edges of the head casing to match the mitered cut on the other side casing. Adjust the miter saw to correspond to that angle, and miter-cut the head casing 1/16 inch. Wedge it into position and nail to ensure a tight fit. If a small gap still exists, tighten it by lock nailing.

INSTALLING BUTT-JOINTED TRIM

Installing flat boards with butt joints as casings simplifies the job, and the result still looks good. For a different look, install moldings for the casing sides and butt-joint them against a flat board for the head.

Another attractive option is to make the head casing wider than the side casings. For example, if you use 1×3 stock for the side casing, use a 1×4 or 1×6 for the head casing. You can also let the ends of the head casing extend beyond the side casings by 1/2 inch to 1 1/2 inches. Round the ends of the head casing with a router or a wood rasp for a more finished look.

Before cutting the tops of the side casings, check that the head jamb is level. If it slopes slightly, adjust the cuts at the tops of the side casings. Use a long level to mark the cuts. Cut the head casing, put in place, and nail.

TWO TIPS FOR TIGHT CORNERS

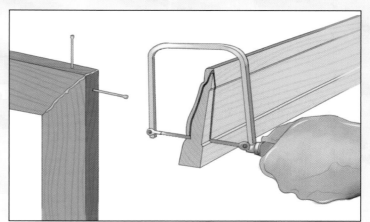

Here are two simple techniques that will give you the tight, gap-free corners that enhance your trim job.

LOCK NAILING
When a mitered joint is off slightly, this method can often be used to close the gap. It works because the trim wood is usually flexible. First squeeze some glue into the crack. Then drive a casing nail through the head casing into the side casing and another nail from the side casing into the head casing, as shown above left. Wipe away any excess glue immediately and sand the joint lightly when dry.

COPING A MITERED JOINT
When you work with molded casing, which may be thick and ornate, the joints must always be mitered so that the molding will stay in a consistent line. For a tight joint, bevel the back of one mitered piece. Turn the casing over and use a coping saw to cut a thick scallop of wood from the back. Coping is necessary on only one side of a mitered joint.

DOORS FOR SPECIAL SITUATIONS

A standard door isn't always what you need; sometimes you need different types of doors. Inside the house, bifold, pocket, and bypass doors save space in tight quarters. Outside, you'll find a true special-purpose door—your home's garage door. Here's a closer look at these doors.

BIFOLD DOORS

In a number of places where a conventional door would just get in the way, a bifold unit might save the day. When open, these doors fold neatly against the jambs. When closed, they can provide a visual break in the wall.

Many bifold doors are louvered—either full-length or on the top half. Louvered doors are handy where you want to allow ventilation, for instance to enclose appliances like a washer and dryer. Others feature panel construction for a classic look. Flush hollow-core bifolds match standard interior doors. Others are made of metal or plastic. A big advantage of bifold doors is that they are easy to install in an existing door frame.

Bifold doors take less space than standard doors when opened. They're great for closets and utility areas.

A bifold unit consists of two doors hinged together. Large openings call for two units of equal size—one at each side of the opening.

Bifolds come in a number of sizes. But if you cannot find doors to fit your openings exactly, you can modify either the doors or the opening. When the doorway is too narrow for the doors, trim the doors equally with a plane or table saw. When the doorway is too wide, you may be able to build up the side jambs with stock that is thick enough to make the doors fit.

The hardware for bifold doors consists of an overhead track that contains a top pivot, a bottom pivot, a slide guide, alignment fingers for double-unit sets, and an adjustable pivot pin for the bottom of the door, which allows you to raise or lower the door.

INSTALLING BIFOLD DOORS

Here are the steps for installing a bifold door. The illustrations on the opposite page show typical hardware. But hardware design can vary, so check your door's instructions.

■ Measure the width of the door opening. If necessary, cut the overhead track to fit with a hacksaw. Place the track along the centerline of the head jamb and mark the centers of the screw holes. Set the track aside and drill the holes in the head jamb.

■ Next insert the rubber bumper on the door closing side of the track. For a pair of doors that close in the middle, slide the bumper to the center of the track so it will cushion the doors when they close. Slip the top pivot bracket onto the hinge end of the track. For a pair of doors, put top pivot brackets on both ends. Then screw the track to the head jamb.

■ Push the top pivot bracket (or brackets) against the sides of the doorway, but don't tighten the holding screw yet.

■ Drop a plumb bob from the end of the track and position the bottom pivot bracket directly under the top one. For a pair of doors, do this at each end.

■ Screw the brackets to the wall and to the floor. If carpeting will be laid, cut a strip of plywood to fit under each bottom bracket as a shim. Make it thick enough to raise the bracket slightly above the carpet.

■ Insert the vertical adjusting bolt into the bottom of each door; drill holes if needed.

■ Drill the top of each door and insert the top pivot and slide guide as shown on the opposite page.

■ Set the door's bottom pivot into the bottom socket. (If there are two door units, install them one at a time.)

BIFOLD DOORS

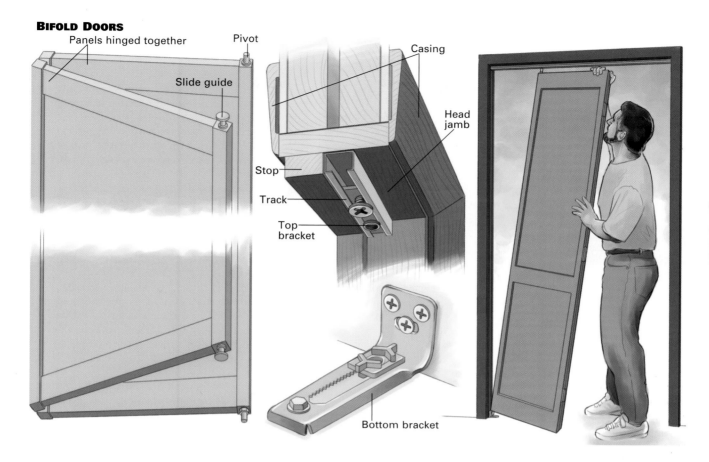

Panels hinged together
Pivot
Slide guide
Casing
Head jamb
Stop
Track
Top bracket
Bottom bracket

■ Slide the top pivot bracket to the middle of the track. Tilt the top of the door toward the center of the opening and fit the door's top pivot into the bracket.

■ Push the bracket and the door back to the jamb side. Make sure that the door is vertical, then tighten the holding screws on the top and bottom brackets.

■ Open the door and raise or lower it as necessary by turning the vertical adjusting bolt. Match the door heights if you are installing a pair.

■ Install the pulls or knobs. On a double-bifold set, close the doors and screw the metal door alignment fingers in place on the back face of each door about 8 inches from the bottom.

■ Trim the door opening.

Bypass sliding doors open only a part of the doorway at a time. But the doors don't need space to swing. They're often the best choice for clothes closets. Installation is covered on the next page.

DOORS FOR SPECIAL SITUATIONS
continued

SLIDING DOORS

Bypass sliding doors are favorites for closets because they require less space than a hinged door, offer reasonable access, are inexpensive, and are easy to install. A disadvantage is that only half the doorway can be open at once.

You can hang virtually any style of door with bypass hardware. Ordinary flush hollow-core doors are the norm, but louvered or paneled doors would also work. You can also find metal-framed, mirrored sliding doors in several standard sizes.

The basic hardware for bypass doors includes an overhead track, a pair of rollers that attach to the top of each door and ride in the track, and a door guide that fastens to the floor. Better quality hardware sets include a floor track with rollers built into it to guide the doors smoothly. The floor track is better for heavy doors—particularly mirrored ones—to reduce rattling. You can buy the hardware separately or buy the doors and the hardware in one kit.

The doors should be 1½ inches shorter than the height of the opening. This allows 1¼ inches at the top for the track and ¼ inch for clearance above the floor or carpet. You can adjust floor clearance by raising or lowering the doors with adjusting screws on the rollers, as illustrated below left.

Both doors should be the same width, each ½ inch wider than half the width of the opening. (Or, the width of the finished opening should be 1 inch less than the total width of the doors.) This allows the doors to overlap by 1 inch when closed.

INSTALLING THE DOOR: Here's the general procedure for installing bypass doors:

■ Fit the track to the head jamb of your opening, following the manufacturer's instructions.

■ Mark the head jamb through the holes in the track, then drill pilot holes for the track attaching screws.

■ Install the track. Place it so the channels that carry the door-hanger rollers face into the closet.

■ Mount a pair of hanger rollers on the top end of each door, about 2 inches in from each edge.

■ Hang the inside door on the inside track channel first. Refer to the hardware manufacturer's instructions for the method of engaging the rollers in the track. Usually you'll have to tilt the door as you lift it into the opening. Then hang the outside door.

■ Close the doors to see how straight they hang by comparing them to the side jambs, which should be plumb. Adjust the doors to meet the side jambs squarely, following the manufacturer's instructions. To adjust the hang of most doors, you turn a screw or move a lever on the hanger roller, as shown at the left.

■ Install the floor guide or, if applicable, the floor track. The guide screws to the floor in the center of the opening. If the guide is adjustable, as most are, set the

BYPASS DOORS

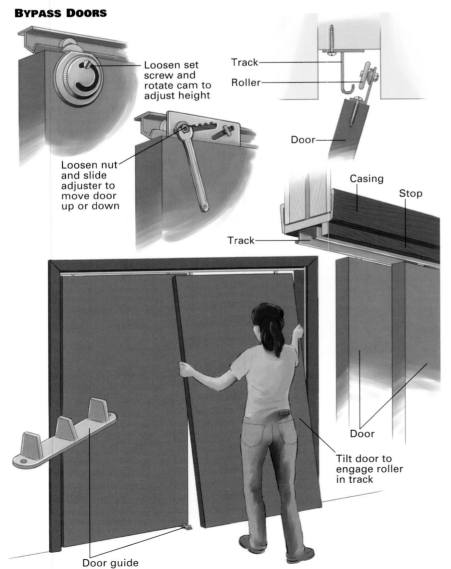

Loosen set screw and rotate cam to adjust height

Loosen nut and slide adjuster to move door up or down

Track

Roller

Door

Casing

Stop

Track

Door

Tilt door to engage roller in track

Door guide

inside and outside fingers to clear the doors by ⅛ inch. Refer to the manufacturer's instructions to mount a floor track.

POCKET DOORS

A pocket door is a sliding door that disappears into the wall. A pocket door offers the main advantage of a sliding door—no need to allow for door swing—but also allows a full opening. The major limitation is that enough wall must be available next to the opening for the door to slide into.

There are two ways to buy a pocket door. You can purchase a complete ready-made unit, or you can buy the hardware for the door of your choice. The ready-made units are sold in a variety of standard widths, all 80 inches high. Pocket-door hardware sets usually include an overhead track and adjustable hangers that attach to the top of the door with rollers that fit into the track. The sets also include a split jamb side and a split stud.

INSTALLING A POCKET DOOR: Putting in a pocket door requires re-covering part of the wall, making it a more ambitious project than installing bifold or bypass doors in an existing opening. But the task is well within the capability of a competent do-it-yourselfer. Here's a general overview of installing a ready-made pocket door in an existing wall:

FRAMING THE ROUGH OPENING:

■ First, determine where you want the door to be. Plan the wall opening so the latch side of the door can go against an existing stud, if possible. Snap a chalk line down the latch side of the opening. Center the chalk line on the stud, if there is one.

■ From the latch side, measure across the wall a distance equal to twice the width of the door opening. Find the nearest stud beyond that point and snap a chalk line down the center of it.

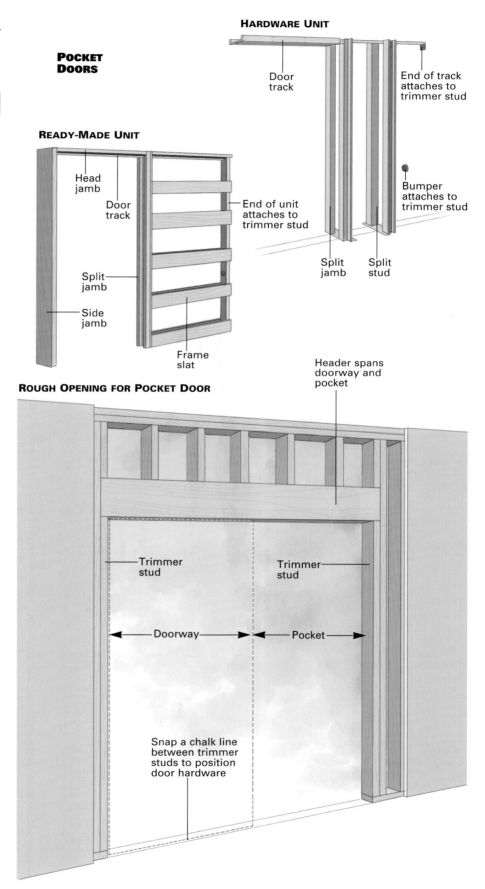

POCKET DOORS

HARDWARE UNIT

Door track

End of track attaches to trimmer stud

Bumper attaches to trimmer stud

Split jamb

Split stud

READY-MADE UNIT

Head jamb

Door track

End of unit attaches to trimmer stud

Split jamb

Side jamb

Frame slat

ROUGH OPENING FOR POCKET DOOR

Header spans doorway and pocket

Trimmer stud

Trimmer stud

Doorway

Pocket

Snap a chalk line between trimmer studs to position door hardware

DOORS FOR SPECIAL SITUATIONS
continued

■ Cut the paneling or wallboard along the chalk lines, and remove the section between the lines. (Refer to page 16 for information on stripping the wall.)

■ Determine whether the wall is a load-bearing wall. If it is, shore it up before you proceed. (Refer to pages 14–17.)

■ If you are installing a pocket door in place of an existing doorway, remove the door jambs and the rough-opening framing, including the header.

■ Remove the wall studs inside the opening. Try to salvage as much as possible of the covering on the other side of the wall. The less damage you do to it now, the less repair work you'll have to do later.

■ Following the procedures described on page 16, cut and fit new king studs, trimmer studs, header, and cripple studs to frame a rough opening of the size required for the pocket-door unit. The bottom of the header should be about 1½ inches above the door so there will be enough room for the track. Plumb and square the opening.

■ Cut away the wall base plate inside the rough opening.

INSTALLING THE DOOR UNIT: The ready-made unit comes with a hollow-core door inside the assembled frame. The head jamb, latch-side jamb, and overhead track are taped to the frame's side slats. Unpack the door, jambs, and track.

■ Slide the assembled pocket frame into the rough opening. Shim it plumb and level, and nail it to the trimmer stud.

■ Cut the door opening through the covering on the other side of the wall.

■ Install the head jamb and latch-side jamb in the opening. Shim the head jamb level, and nail it to the header through the shims for rigidity. Nail the latch-side jamb to the trimmer stud.

■ Position the overhead track on the head jamb, mark the screw-hole centers, and drill pilot holes in the head jamb. Attach the track to the head jamb.

■ Install the door pull and latch assembly.

■ Mount the roller-hanger assemblies on the top of the door, about 1 inch from each edge.

■ Lift the door into place and engage the rollers in the track. Adjust the hangers until the door just clears the floor or carpet and hangs straight when closed.

■ Install the latch strike plate in the jamb.

■ Replace the wallboard or paneling on the wall. Patch the wall as necessary on the other side, and attach it to the framing.

■ Install casing on both sides of the opening.

LOCKS FOR ENTRY DOORS

■ An entry door is only as secure as its lock. A standard latch—with a spring-loaded bolt that has a beveled end—is convenient when you want to pull the door shut behind you. But a burglar can easily force one open. A dead bolt or other auxiliary lock can thwart forced entry. Here are some other ways to enhance security of entry doors:

■ Door latches and dead bolts engage strike plates set into the jamb. If the strike plate fails, the lock gives way. For more security, install heavy-duty strike plates with screws long enough to penetrate into the studs behind the jamb.

■ Burglars don't like to be seen by neighbors, so they might try to get in through your less visible back door. Make it at least as secure as your front door. Be sure it has a solid core, and reinforce the jambs, stops, strike plate, and hinges.

■ Avoid double-cylinder locks, which open from the inside only with a key. They make escape more difficult in emergencies, such as a fire. If you are considering one because the door has glass panes, either replace the door or install smashproof polycarbonate plastic in place of the glass. Then install a single-cylinder dead-bolt lock.

INSTALLING A CYLINDER LOCK

Mark hole centers on door from lock manufacturer's template, then bore holes

Insert lock backset in door, and scribe around the faceplate

Install lock

Chisel shallow mortise for faceplate

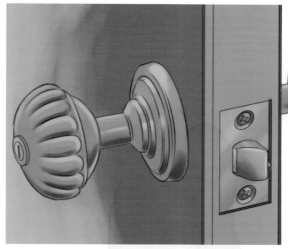

Cylinder Lock

A cylinder lock, also known as a tubular or key-in-knob lock, fits into a hole drilled through the door, so it's easy to install. This, along with its low cost, makes it the most popular type of lock. It is also the easiest lock to force open, so it is often installed with an auxiliary dead-bolt lock. Matching-key lock and dead-bolt sets are easy to find.

Dead-Bolt Lock

A dead bolt added to a door increases security. The throw bolt should extend at least 1 inch into the jamb because prying open a door will usually force the lock no more than ½ inch. The lock is difficult to jimmy from the outside because it is either flush with the door surface or protrudes as a tapered cylinder, often freely revolving. It's relatively easy to install.

Mortise Lock

Combining a latch and a dead bolt, this unit offers greater security than the cylinder lock alone. But it is difficult to install, and the mortise that houses the mechanism weakens the door. This was the most common type of lock years ago. Today many high-quality entry handle locks are mortise locks.

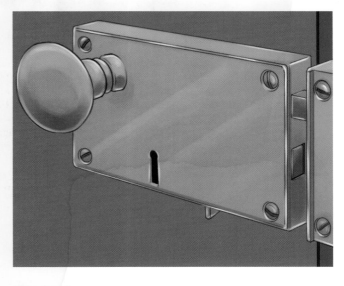

Rim Lock

Like the dead bolt, this lock is installed along with a key latch to augment security. It fastens to the inside surface of the door, so is more visible than a dead bolt and easier to install. The strike plate secures to the casing as well as to the rim of the jamb. This type of lock is strong and highly resistant to jimmying.

STORM AND SCREEN DOORS

A storm door creates an insulating dead-air space in front of an exterior door and keeps wind, rain, and snow away from the door. In warm weather, screen doors allow ventilation while keeping insects outside. These lightweight doors are structurally similar and are installed in the same manner.

CHOOSING STORM AND SCREEN DOORS

Storm doors are made of wood, metal, or clad wood. Some are insulated. When you go shopping for one, you'll find three varieties: Those that have fixed glazing, combination doors that have interchangeable glazed and screened inserts, and self-storing combination doors, in which a glazed panel slides closed behind a fixed screen for storm protection.

Metal-framed storm doors with fixed glazing are widely available with full-length glazing that won't hide an attractive entry door. Since these doors are often double-glazed, the entry door can be left open on mild days while the storm door holds back the chill and lets in the light.

Combination doors allow you to change quickly from a storm door in the winter to a screen door the rest of the year, but you'll have to store each insert during its off season. Self-storing combination doors avoid this problem—the glazed storm window simply slides out of the way of the screen. You don't have to remove and store it.

The traditional screen door started to fall from favor as residential air-conditioning and combination doors became more common. But in mild climates, a screen door still makes a good choice. And some older home styles, particularly those with broad porches, often don't look quite right without a screen door in the summer. Screen doors, which are almost always made of wood, range from plain and simple to ornate Victorian styles.

INSTALLING COMBINATION DOORS: Metal and clad combination (and self-storing combination) doors are usually sold as ready-to-install units with jambs and hardware. The same is true of metal-framed storm doors with fixed glazing. These door units are designed to attach directly to the brick molding around an exterior door, making installation a relatively simple matter. Here's the usual installation procedure:

■ Measure the width and height of the opening. Storm doors usually allow a little leeway in sizing, so the one you buy may not fit your opening precisely. The manufacturer's instructions will explain how to properly fit it to your opening. When you take the measurements, also note whether the entry door's knob is on the right or left side; you'll want to buy a storm door with the knob on the opposite side.

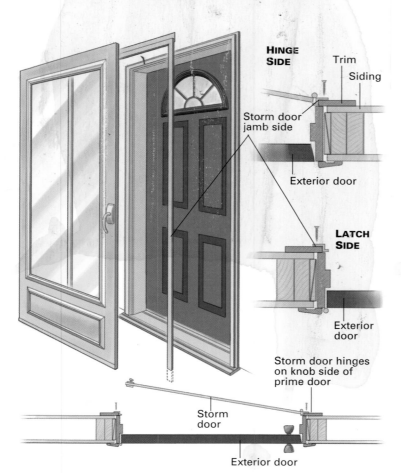

HINGE SIDE

Trim

Siding

Storm door jamb side

Exterior door

LATCH SIDE

Exterior door

Storm door hinges on knob side of prime door

Storm door

Exterior door

■ Trim the jamb sides to the height of your opening. Cut the bottom ends of the jamb sides at an angle to match the slope of the sill. A hacksaw with 24 or 32 teeth per inch will cut the aluminum members easily.

■ Position the unit in the opening and center it. The narrow jambs fit over the face and inside edge of the brick mold along the sides and across the top of the opening. Most manufacturers include instructions to help you determine whether you need to place filler strips between the jamb sides and the brick molding.

■ Drill screw holes through the jamb sides and head, following the manufacturer's recommendations for size, location, and spacing.

■ Position the door in the opening, center it, and plumb it. Drill screw pilot holes in the brick mold, centered in the jamb holes. Drive in the screws provided or recommended by the manufacturer to secure the door.

■ If not already done, install the latch on the door. Install the closer and the latch strike plate. Adjust the bottom door sweep.

INSTALLING A SCREEN DOOR: Wooden screen doors and combination doors that aren't prehung call for a different procedure:

■ Measure the opening and check it for square. Test it by holding a framing square at both the top and bottom corners along the side that will be the hinge side of the opening. Check the hinge side for plumb.

If the opening is far out of square or the hinge side is far out of plumb, fix the problem before trying to hang the door. You can make up for small deviations when you trim the door to fit.

■ Cut the door to ¼ inch less than the door opening in both height and width. This will allow ⅛-inch clearance on each side and along the top and bottom.

■ Test the door's fit in the opening. Mark the edge of the door on the hinge side.

■ Attach a pair of surface-mount screen-door hinges to the outside face of the door on the hinge side. Spring hinges are the best kind to use; they'll help close the door and reduce its rattling somewhat. Hinge placement is not critical; common practice is to put the top of one 7 inches from the top of the door and the bottom of the other 11 inches from the door bottom. For a door that will see a lot of traffic, center a third hinge between the two.

■ Place the door in the opening and center it with shims. Lay the hinge leaves against the face of the brick mold and mark the screw positions.

■ Drill screw pilot holes. Screw the hinges to the molding.

■ Close the door, wedge it shut, and check the gap all around. Plane the door along the latch edge, top, or bottom as needed to create an equal gap of ⅛ to 3/16 inch all around.

■ Install the latch or handle. For a knob or lever latch, drill holes where indicated by the hardware instructions. Install the latch on the door and the strike plate on the jamb.

■ On a full-screen door—one without a wood panel in the lower half to stiffen it—install a screen-door brace (a pair of long rods connected by a turnbuckle). Attach the top of the brace on the inside of the door near the hinge edge. Screw the bottom to the lower corner of the door along the latch edge.

GARAGE DOORS

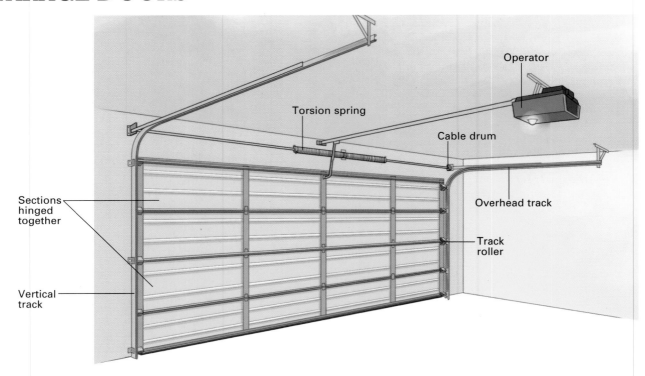

Operator

Torsion spring

Cable drum

Sections
hinged
together

Overhead track

Track
roller

Vertical
track

M ost homes today have overhead
garage doors, either sectional or
trackless. Sectional doors are
constructed of several horizontal panels,
hinged together, that roll up on tracks.
Trackless doors have one panel that swings
out and up on arms.

Measure the opening to determine the door
size. Also measure the distances from the sides
of the opening to the garage sidewalls and
ceiling. You'll need all of these dimensions in
order to make sure there is enough room for
the tracks and the opener equipment. Special
low-overhead installation kits are often
available to install sectional doors where
the ceiling is low.

Many companies can provide a custom
garage door to match the architecture of your
house. With the range of door styles available,
you'll probably be able to find or order exactly
what you want.

Garage doors are available in standard
or custom sizes. Standard sizes are most
economical and fit most modern garages.
If you live in an older home, you may need a
custom-size door: Garages built before World
War II were small, designed to accommodate
the taller, narrow cars of that era, and had
narrow doors. You might be able to alter your
door opening to accept a standard door, but
this may not be feasible in some garages.

If you do plan to widen the garage door
opening, it is important to have a strong
enough header to span the opening. Consult
a professional to determine what size header
you need. See the section on structural
preparations and shoring (pages 12–17) for
advice on supporting the garage wall for work.

DANGER IN SPRINGS

Springs help lift an overhead garage door and
hold it open. They may be torsion springs,
which exert a twisting force, or extension
springs, which simply stretch. The springs
on an existing door may be under great
tension. Be careful when removing or
attempting to repair an existing door; the
springs can cause serious injury.

A torsion spring, usually identifiable as a
cylindrical spring on a shaft running across
the top of the door opening, is under high
tension. Only a professional should work on
one. Extension springs are safer for a do-it-
yourselfer to handle but should still be
handled carefully. Even a spring that seems
loose can be storing a lot of energy.

INSTALLING A GARAGE DOOR

Garage doors are easy for a pair of workers to install, if you follow the manufacturer's instructions. Most manufacturers also offer free technical help via a toll-free telephone number. You'll usually perform these steps to install a sectional door:

■ Assemble the track sections, attach them to the framing alongside the door opening, and suspend the overhead portion from the ceiling framing.

■ Attach hinge and roller hardware to the door sections.

■ Place the lower section in the opening, and fit it to the garage floor.

■ Place the remaining door sections into the opening one at a time, fitting the rollers into the track and attaching each piece to the section below.

■ Connect the cables, pulleys, and springs. Install the lock and other hardware. Tension the springs.

■ Trim the door opening, and apply the weather stripping.

■ Install and test the opener.

The garage door and trim should harmonize with the house.

GARAGE DOOR TRIM

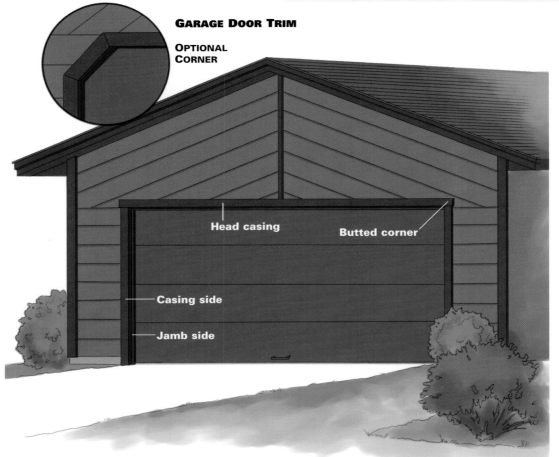

OPTIONAL
CORNER

Head casing

Butted corner

Casing side

Jamb side

DOOR TROUBLESHOOTING

You can get used to a door that doesn't work right because it just seems like a lot of trouble to fix it. But many door problems are easy to fix, and letting them go can damage the door and the jambs. Also, some problems will cost you in energy loss.

STICKING DOORS

A door may stick when humidity swells the wood, worn or unlubricated hinges bind, loose hinge screws allow the door to sag, or loose joints in the door itself cause it to sag.

SWOLLEN WOOD: Expansion of the wood during a damp or humid period can cause a door to stick. If you plane it down to fit while it is swollen, however, it will often end up too loose during the dry season when it shrinks. You will have to judge whether it sticks badly enough to justify planing it. If it just binds slightly, rubbing a little soap on the sticking point will probably help.

A good finish on the door can minimize seasonal swelling and shrinking. Paint or a clear finish, such as polyurethane, varnish, lacquer, or shellac, can reduce moisture absorption by the wood. Stain alone offers no protection. You have to finish both faces, the top, bottom, and both edges. A door finished on one side only is likely to warp.

FIXING HINGES: If the door tends to stick year-round, the problem could be the hinges.

Open the door and make sure all the hinge screws are tight. Loose hinges let the door sag, causing it to stick. Drive in the loose screws. If one won't tighten because the wood around it has been stripped out, remove the screw, then coat a wooden match or a piece of scrap wood with glue and push it into the hole. Cut the plug flush with the surface after the glue has dried. Drive the screw into the repaired screw hole.

If the door sticks and the hinges are all tight, close the door and stand back to inspect the gap on the latch side. Shim out the hinge wherever the gap is wider—at the top or bottom. To do that, loosen the screws in the leaf of the hinge on the jamb, cut a piece of cardboard the height of the hinge leaf about ¼ inch wide, slip it behind the leaf, and retighten the screw.

Shimming involves trial and error. Another method of adjusting the hinges eliminates the need for shimming. Remove the hinge pin, and insert shims between the door and the threshold until the door is straight in the jamb. Then with a pair of pliers, bend the knuckles of the hinge leaf attached to the jamb until they line up with those on the door. Protect the hinge from the pliers with

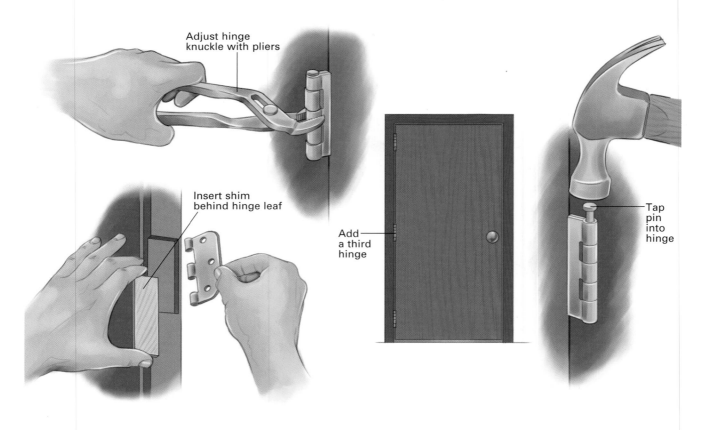

Adjust hinge knuckle with pliers

Insert shim behind hinge leaf

Add a third hinge

Tap pin into hinge

duct tape or cardboard. Reinsert the pin. You can usually move the door about ⅛ inch this way without binding any other hinges.

Hinges on heavy exterior doors eventually wear, causing the door to sag. This can even occur on interior doors. Signs of wear are elongated holes in the hinge knuckles or worn spots on the hinge pin. Replace the worn hinges.

For a heavy or often-used door, consider installing heavy-duty, ball-bearing hinges. You may not find these on the shelf at your local lumberyard or home improvement center—they're more commonly installed in commercial buildings than homes. A lumberyard or hardware dealer should be able to order them for you. These hinges may be made of heavier metal than your existing hinges, calling for deeper mortises in the door and jamb.

REPAIRING DAMAGED DOORS

PATCHING A HOLLOW-CORE DOOR:
A hard hit can leave a hole in a hollow-core door. After you pull away the splintered wood, you can repair a painted door (or one you're willing to paint) this way.

Lightly sand the edge of the hole. Then wad up a sheet of newspaper, coat the back of it with glue, and push it into the hole. Spread a layer of wallboard patching compound over the hole and let it dry overnight. Then apply another coat, bringing it out flush with the surface of the door. (The patching compound may shrink or crack if you try to fill the hole with one thick layer.) Let the repair dry completely, then sand it smooth and paint the door.

FIXING A SPLINTERED DOOR:
The top or bottom edge of a veneered door may become splintered from rubbing against the jamb or floor or being kicked or hit. Dampness can loosen and wrinkle the veneer, too.

To repair this damage, clean out any dried glue, wood chips, or dirt in the spot. Squirt some white glue under the splintered area and spread it around with the corner of a business card or matchbook. Press the veneer back down and wipe off the excess glue. Lay waxed paper over the repair, then put a piece of scrap plywood about the size of the glued area over the waxed paper. Clamp the plywood to the door, protecting the other side from the clamp with a piece of scrap wood.

If a chunk of wood is missing from the door, fill the spot with wood putty. To repair an area more than ⅛ inch deep, fill it to half its depth, let it dry overnight, then apply more putty. Sand when dry, then paint or stain to match the door.

PATCHING A HOLLOW-CORE DOOR

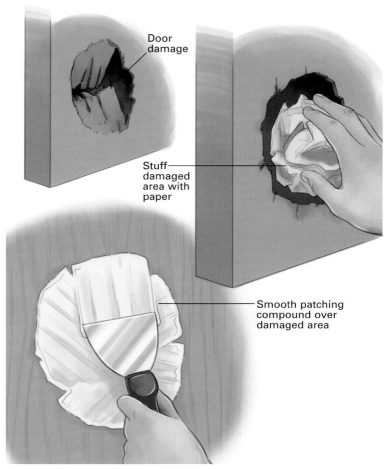

Door damage

Stuff damaged area with paper

Smooth patching compound over damaged area

FIXING A SPLINTERED DOOR

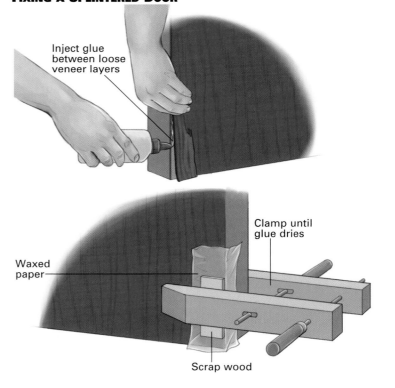

Inject glue between loose veneer layers

Clamp until glue dries

Waxed paper

Scrap wood

DOOR TROUBLESHOOTING
continued

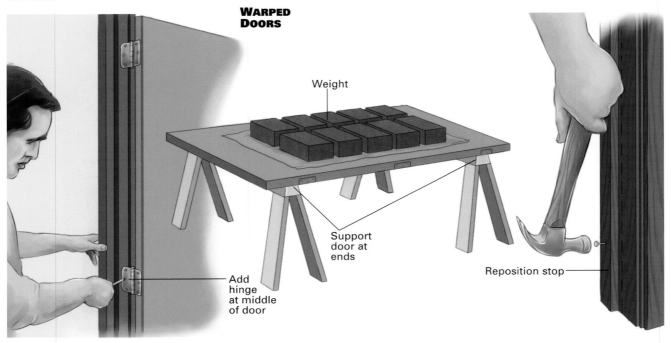

WARPED DOORS

Weight

Support door at ends

Add hinge at middle of door

Reposition stop

SANDING AND PLANING: A little sanding or planing will often cure a sticking wooden door. A plane is the traditional tool for fixing a sticking door. Sanding is slow, but works fine when you need to remove only a small amount of wood.

The first step is to find out just where the door is sticking. Start by looking for telltale scuff marks on the jamb or door edge. Check the latch and its strike plate, too. To test for sticking spots, slip a piece of typing paper between the door edge and the jamb, then swing the door as you slide the paper along the edge. Wherever the paper gets caught, the door is binding.

For minor sticking along the latch edge of the door, wedge the door open with a doorstop or shims. Then plane or sand the edge until the door swings freely. Remove enough wood to allow finishing.

For more extensive fitting, remove the hinge pins, bottom hinge first, and remove the door from the opening. You'll need a helper if the door is heavy. Secure the door in door bucks, by clamping it to a suitable work support, or by pushing one end into a corner of the room to brace it.

Remove the latch hardware if you'll be planing in that area. When planing the latch edge, maintain a slight bevel (about 5 degrees) from the outside to the inside. This helps reduce binding when the door opens and closes. When planing the top or bottom of the door, start at the edges and plane toward the center. Planing from the center to the edge will splinter or tear out the edge.

If you want to sand rather than plane, wrap the sandpaper around a block of wood to keep it flat on the edge of the door. Start with a coarse sandpaper—80-grit or so—to remove wood quickly. Smooth the sanded area for finishing by sanding with 100-, 180-, then 220-grit paper.

STRAIGHTENING A WARPED DOOR: Warping or bowing can render a door nearly useless. In some cases, such as when a door matches others and would be difficult or expensive to replace, you may want to try straightening the door instead of throwing it away.

When a door is only slightly out of true, a simple solution is to move the door stops in the jamb to conform to the door. You can only do this, of course, where the stops are nailed on, not with a rabbeted jamb.

To move the stop, tap a knife or flat trowel along the joint between the stop and jamb on both sides to pop it loose. Carefully pry the stop from the jamb with a flat pry bar and remove the nails. Then close the door, press the stop against the door face along the edge, and nail it into place.

If the door is bowed in the middle, try straightening it with weights. Lay the door on a pair of sawhorses or chairs, the bulge facing up. Then place heavy objects—books or bricks—in the center until the weight straightens it out.

If the door is twisted, try pulling it true with a couple of lengths of wire and a turnbuckle, available at hardware stores. First drive in a screw eye at each corner diagonally across the warp. Attach the wires to the screw hooks and the turnbuckle. Set a short length of 2×4 on edge in the center of the warp with wire stretched over it to provide more leverage. Then tighten the turnbuckle. Increase the tension daily over a period of three or four days. Tightening it all at once may pull the screw eyes out. Once the door is straight, remove the screw hook and fill the holes.

Sand and refinish the door after straightening it. This will reduce the chance of it warping again. Both faces, the top, bottom, and edges must be finished.

SAWING A DOOR

If you need to remove more than ¼ inch from a door—so it will fit into a new opening or clear a new threshold, for instance—make the cut perfectly straight. Avoid splintering when cutting across the grain, such as at the bottom of a veneered door. If you make the cut with a portable circular saw, place the door's best face down.

Here's how to make a straight, accurate cut on a door with a circular saw:
■ Install a sharp, fine-toothed blade on your saw. A carbide-tipped blade with 30 or more teeth (on a 7¼-inch diameter blade) would be a good choice.
■ Draw a line on the back face of the door where you want to make the cut.
■ For a cross-grain cut, score the line with a sharp utility knife to sever the wood fibers. This will lessen splintering when you make the cut. Transfer the line to the other side of the door, and score it, too.
■ Lay a straight-edged board on the door to guide the saw. (The factory edge of a piece of plywood makes a good straightedge.) It's best if it extends far enough past the door to guide the saw into and out of the cut. Make the guide wide enough that you'll be able to clamp it to the door without putting clamps in the way of the saw.
■ Set the saw at one end of the cutting line, positioning it to cut just slightly on the waste side of the line. Slide one end of the guide up against the saw base, and clamp the guide to the door. Measure the distance from the line to the guide, and set the other end of the guide that distance from the line.
■ Hold the saw base firmly against the guide as you make the cut. Move the saw steadily across the door without forcing it.

The solid-wood filler at the bottom of a hollow-core door extends only an inch or so up into the door. You may cut it away altogether when you saw off a hollow-core door. If that happens, peel the veneer faces from the wood filler, using a chisel and mallet. Then slice the cardboard honeycomb filler free of the inside door faces with a knife or chisel, going far enough into the door to make room for the wood filler. Glue the filler into place, clamping it until the glue dries.
■ Sand or plane the cut edge to remove any saw marks. Sand or plane a slight chamfer on each face of the door to prevent splintering.

MAKE A JIG FOR STRAIGHT CUTS

If you have many doors to cut, the sawing jig shown at the bottom of the page will save time. Start with a piece of ¼-inch hardboard or plywood about 7 feet long and 24 inches wide. Cut another piece to the same length and 12 inches wide. Glue this piece along the center of the first piece.

Next set your circular saw for a 90-degree cut. (Check it with a try square.) Set the saw on the jig with its base riding against the guide down the middle. Cut along one side of the jig. Tilt the saw to a 5-degree angle—the angle for the latch-side bevel on a door— and saw along the other edge of the jig. The edge of the jig now shows exactly where the saw will cut. Just lay the jig on the door, place its edge along the cutting line, and clamp it in place.

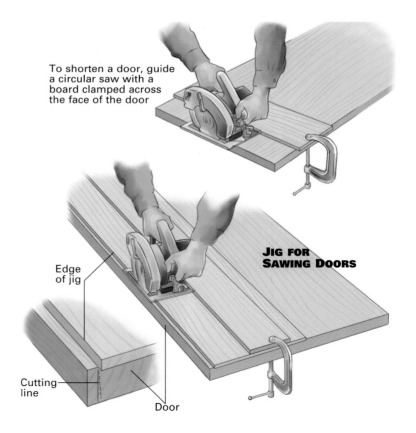

To shorten a door, guide a circular saw with a board clamped across the face of the door

JIG FOR SAWING DOORS

Edge of jig

Cutting line

Door

DOOR TROUBLESHOOTING
continued

REPLACING A THRESHOLD

Most thresholds are made of hardwood and take years of wear. Some are aluminum. Eventually all thresholds show their age and need replacing. Here's what's involved:

First see how the threshold is installed. Does it butt against the doorjambs at its ends or does it extend under the jambs? Most aluminum ones and some wood ones fit the first example, and removal is simple. You might need to remove the door stops, then you can remove the screws from an aluminum threshold or pry up a wooden one with a thin pry bar.

Most wood thresholds extend under the jambs. In this case, saw through the threshold just inside the stops on each jamb side. (You can leave the stops in place.) Pry up the center section, then knock the end pieces out from under the jambs with a mallet and chisel. Do as little damage as possible to the pieces so you can use them as a pattern for cutting the new threshold. If that isn't possible, measure the opening carefully and cut a cardboard pattern to fit.

Cut the new threshold and tap it into position. Protect the wood from the hammer with a piece of scrap wood. Don't force the threshold or you may damage the jambs. Instead plane or sand the ends where they fit under the jamb. If one end is low, shim it with strips of felt paper. Once you have a good fit, remove the threshold and lay three thick beads of caulk on the subfloor.

Drill holes for nails or screws, then attach the threshold to the floor. If you install it with screws, countersink the heads and fill the holes.

FIXING DENTS IN METAL DOORS

Metal doors are durable, but a sharp blow can leave a dent. For the best way to fix your particular door, consult the manufacturer or dealer.

You can fill minor dents with body filler, available at auto-parts stores. To do this, sand the area down to bare metal. Mix some filler, following the instructions on the package. Spread it over the damaged area with a putty knife or plastic spreader. Apply several thin layers instead of one thick one. When the final layer is partially cured, shave it flush with the door surface, using a Surform plane. Sand when dry and repaint the door.

FIXING A SAGGING SCREEN DOOR

Screen doors often sag because they come apart

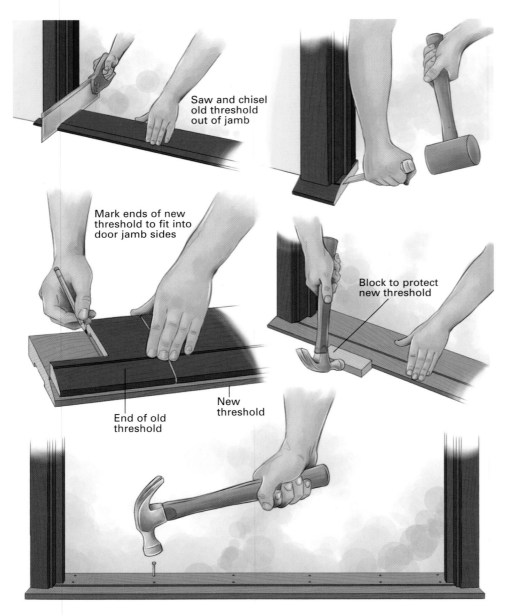

Saw and chisel old threshold out of jamb

Mark ends of new threshold to fit into door jamb sides

End of old threshold

New threshold

Block to protect new threshold

REPAIRING A SCREEN

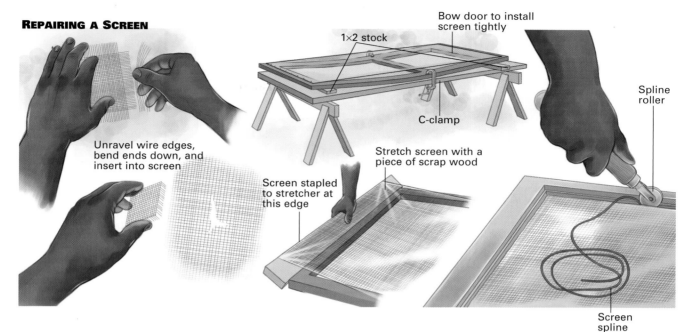

Unravel wire edges, bend ends down, and insert into screen

Bow door to install screen tightly

1×2 stock

C-clamp

Spline roller

Stretch screen with a piece of scrap wood

Screen stapled to stretcher at this edge

Screen spline

at the joints. To fix this, pry the joint apart slightly, inject some glue, and clamp it. (A weather-resistant glue, such as polyurethane or waterproof woodworker's glue, would be the best choice here.) Then drill through the stiles into the ends of the rails, and drive in long wood screws.

A diagonal brace running between the top corner on the hinge side and the bottom corner on the latch side can both cure and prevent screen-door sag. Attach two T-braces as shown below right and connect them with steel wire or cable. Install a turnbuckle near one corner to pull the wire tight and keep it that way.

SCREEN REPLACEMENT: Torn or loose screening can be patched temporarily, but the best fix is to replace it with new screening.

■ For a wooden screen door, remove the moldings around the screen (the screen bead) and pull out the staples holding the screening in place. Be careful when removing the screen bead so you can reuse it.

Buy a piece of steel wire screening a few inches wider than your door's opening and about 6 inches longer. Lay it in place and staple it across the bottom of the opening using a standard staple gun.

To stretch the screen tight, lay boards under the ends of the door as shown above, then clamp the middle to your work surface. You don't have to bow the door much. Pull the screen tight and staple it across the top of the opening. Unclamp the door and staple the screen along the sides. Trim the excess screen with a utility knife, then reinstall the screen bead.

■ A rubber or plastic spline usually holds the screen in place in a metal frame. To replace the screen, pry one end of the spline loose with an awl or knife, then pull it out of

the groove around the opening. Cut a piece of fiberglass or aluminum screening a few inches larger than the opening in both directions. When you buy the screening, take the old spline along as a match, and buy a new piece. (It's usually easiest to replace screening with the same kind—fiberglass or aluminum—that came out of the frame.)

Press the spline and screening into the groove along the bottom of the opening, using the roller tool made for the job. (You can buy one where you buy the screening.) Be careful not to let the roller slip off the spline onto the screen—it will cut through the screen. Stretch the screen as you work your way around the opening. Trim the end of the spline at the end, then cut away the excess screen around the opening.

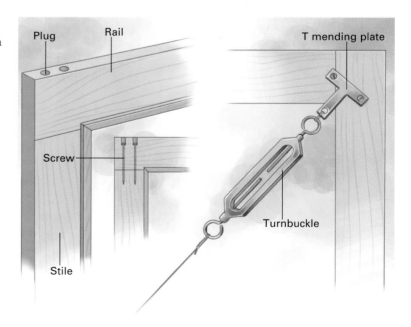

Plug

Rail

T mending plate

Screw

Turnbuckle

Stile

WINDOWS

Windows have the power to transform a house. New windows can update the appearance of your home or change its style completely, while providing additional natural light and improved energy efficiency. This section shows the many window options available today and provides information about installing them yourself.

Windows have a strong presence in both of these rooms. A wall of windows lets plenty of light into the large room and displays a panoramic view. A trio of generously sized windows, shown below, brightens a small library and home office added above a garage.

FORM AND FUNCTION

For construction economy, your home originally may have been fitted with functional but less-than-stylish windows. Perhaps you want to install new, more energy-efficient windows. Or maybe you just want to see a view or bring more light into an area that's too dark. Whatever your reason for installing new windows, the options offered by manufacturers today are limited only by your imagination and budget. Choosing and buying new windows can be a daunting task. This chapter will show you what's available and how to install windows.

CHOOSING THE STYLE

If you're adding a new window or two, or replacing only some of the windows in your home, make sure that the style of the new windows harmonizes with the ones you want to keep. If you're replacing them all, select a window style that complements your home. Here are some popular types of windows:

■ Double-hung windows feature two sashes that move past each other vertically. Older double-hung windows had sash weights and cords to counterbalance the sash; spring devices replace the cords and weights in newer windows. Sashes on some models tilt into the room, making cleaning much easier. Double-hung windows were notorious for sticking and letting in drafts, but newer ones slide more freely and provide more efficient weather stripping. They are attractive, but generally don't mix well with other styles.
■ Single-hung windows are similar to double-hung ones, except that only the lower sash opens; the upper one is fixed.
■ Sliding windows are popular and are frequently installed in newer buildings. In this type, one sash (or one at each end of a larger unit) slides open horizontally. This, too, is a style that doesn't mix well with others.

Some less costly sliding windows may be of low quality, but good ones can be had, so shop around. In the best windows, tracks and hardware operate smoothly and weather stripping effectively seals out drafts. Sliding windows are usually available in metal and vinyl, although wood ones are made.
■ Casement windows are hinged on the left or right side and open outward. Modern casement windows usually open by turning a crank. Like sliding windows, casements are sometimes placed at each end of a large fixed pane to create a combination window unit.
■ Awning windows are hinged at the top and open outward. Placed high on a wall, they can provide light and ventilation while maintaining privacy. A similar style, the hopper window, opens inward and is usually hinged at the bottom or on a sliding hinge. Hopper windows are frequently installed for basement light and ventilation.
■ Jalousie windows, metal-framed units featuring louverlike slats of glass, are perennial favorites for beach houses, enclosed porches, sunrooms, and similar installations. They're also available as door inserts. The louvers crank open and closed, but jalousie windows can be drafty when closed, so they aren't often installed as prime windows in homes.
■ Fixed-pane windows range in size from small ones made to install in

Multiple windows of standard sizes create a pattern in this wall .

doors—called door lights—to large picture or panorama windows. Fixed-pane windows can be combined with operating windows to create striking effects.

■ Bow and bay windows, composite units made up of several smaller windows, extend outward from a wall for a spacious effect. Bow windows usually comprise four or more windows that form a curve.

A bay window features straight side panes, normally placed at a 30-, 45- or 90-degree angle to the wall, flanking a straight front window that stands parallel to the wall. Either style can incorporate a sill-height window seat or extend to the floor. On the outside, they can be roofed or extend to the soffit.

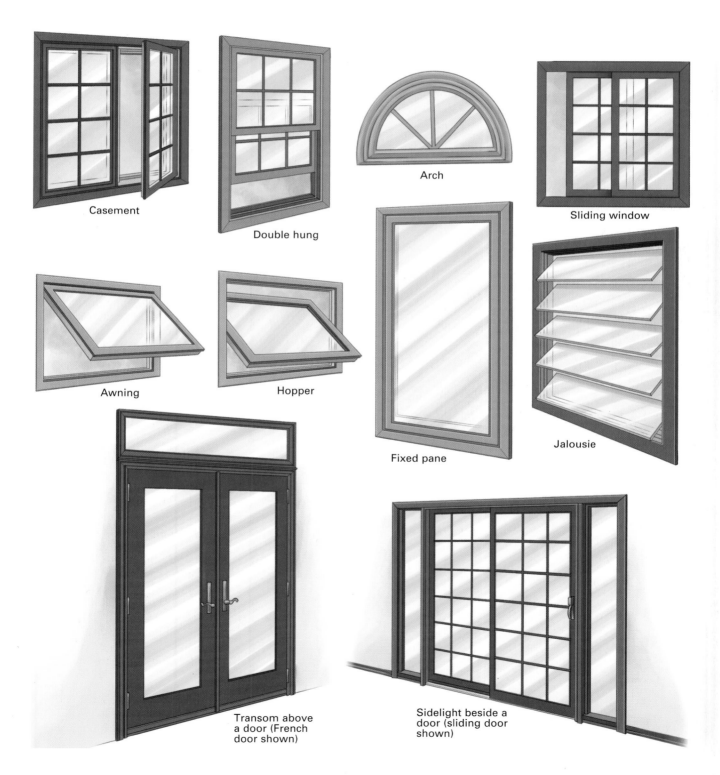

Casement

Double hung

Arch

Sliding window

Awning

Hopper

Fixed pane

Jalousie

Transom above a door (French door shown)

Sidelight beside a door (sliding door shown)

FORM AND FUNCTION
continued

Windows glazed with acrylic blocks let in light and maintain privacy. Awning, casement, and fixed windows are available with the blocks.

LIGHT, VENTILATION, AND PLACEMENT

Climate and exposure are important considerations when you're deciding on new windows. If you live in a rainy climate and like to keep windows open for ventilation, for instance, awning windows could be a good choice. Similarly, casement windows can be oriented so that when they are open, they either scoop air into the room or protect the opening from a prevailing breeze. All opening windows should have screens, of course.

Windows admit sunlight as well as air. Some types control the amount and kind of light they admit. Coatings for glass can keep out damaging UV radiation and help reduce heat loss through the windows. These coatings are discussed on pages 54 and 55.

Consider solar gain when you plan new windows. Modern units keep heat in; you may be surprised at how warm your house can be with thoughtfully placed energy-efficient windows. This can be enhanced by placing the windows so the sun strikes a heat-absorbing surface, which can then radiate the heat into the house at night. A tile floor, particularly one with a few inches of concrete under it, would be one such surface.

Consider the placement of the windows with respect to compass orientation and eaves overhang, too. South windows admit low winter sun, warming the house. They are usually best for plants, too. Shading by the roof overhang, awnings, or landscaping can hold intense summer sun at bay.

East windows admit morning sun. They can cause overheating in summer, yet provide limited heat gain in winter. West windows will be affected most by summer heat, and northern windows are most likely to cause heat loss. Eaves can work to your advantage if you place the windows so that the overhang blocks the high, hot summer sun, but allows the low winter sunlight to warm the interior of the house.

Check the local building code. As an energy-conservation measure, some codes limit the amount of window area you can add to your home or set a maximum glazing area based on the square footage of the house.

SECURITY

If you are buying sliding wood or metal windows, make sure the locking hardware is sturdy. Also make sure that the sash can't be lifted out of the track.

Casement, awning, and hopper windows usually have stout latching devices. Most are not easy to pry open without actually breaking the sash or the glass.

Avoid placing small panes of glass in locations that would allow a person to reach through and open a door or window. Some sidestep this danger by installing a double-cylinder dead-bolt lock—the kind operated by a key from either side—on an entry door. But this poses danger in case of a fire, and violates most safety codes.

A better solution is to install break-resistant plastic glazing. Tempered glass, too, provides some security—it is harder to break and makes a noise when it is smashed. Glass or acrylic block is another option where it can be installed attractively.

SAFETY

Building codes require shatterproof glazing— plastic, tempered glass, or laminated safety glass— in certain installations, including windows less than 18 inches from the floor or within 24 inches of a door. Doors, including storm doors, also require safety glazing. It's also a good idea to put safety glazing wherever someone might bump into or fall against a window, even if it isn't required.

In addition to plastics such as Lexan, two kinds of glass meet safety requirements:

■ Tempered glass is heat-treated and shatters into tiny, relatively harmless bits. (It will shatter if you try to cut it, too. Order the correct size from your glass dealer.)

■ Laminated safety glass is made with a flexible plastic layer sandwiched between two sheets of glass, as in an automobile windshield. If the window breaks, the sharp shards stick to the plastic.

Building codes specify minimum dimensions for windows in rooms where people sleep. A typical requirement calls for each bedroom to have at least one window with a minimum clear opening height of 24 inches and a minimum clear opening width of 20 inches—big enough for a person to fit through to escape a fire. The sill must not be more than 44 inches above the floor. Security grilles are also restricted. Check your local building code for more information on these safety requirements.

Fire safety codes may also forbid you to cut new windows into a wall facing a property line unless the wall is a prescribed distance from the line. Or windows might be permitted in such walls if they carry a fire rating. This is a complex issue that varies widely from place to place; refer to your local building-ode authority.

Traditional eight-over-eight, double-hung windows (two sashes with eight panes in each) fit this Arts and Crafts room style perfectly.

Casement windows blend into this more contemporary-style kitchen.

MATERIALS AND CONSTRUCTION

FRAMES

Wood, vinyl, and aluminum are the most common materials for window frames today. The same window style is often available in several materials from one manufacturer. When examining windows made of any material by any manufacturer, look for smooth-working sashes and hardware.

Wood: The first window frames were made of wood. And wood remains popular, thanks to such advantages as natural insulating qualities and inherent beauty. A major drawback of wood windows has always been the need to protect them from the weather with frequent painting. Some wood-framed windows now come with vinyl or aluminum cladding for a no-maintenance exterior. Aluminum looks a bit crisper but doesn't resist pitting as well as vinyl when exposed to salt water or salt air. Natural wood interior faces of many clad windows can be stained or painted. Manufacturers often treat wood with fungicides or preservatives for durability. Wood windows generally cost more than vinyl or aluminum.

Vinyl: Durable, affordable, energy-efficient vinyl windows have steadily gained in popularity since they first appeared in the 1970s. Easy fabrication makes vinyl a leading choice for custom-size replacement windows. Heat-welded corner joints are strongest. Most vinyl windows come in white; painting them another color is difficult.

Aluminum: Aluminum windows, available in a wide range of styles and quality grades, are both durable and inexpensive. They come standard in mill finish, a raw-metal color, but most manufacturers offer factory-applied coatings in a limited range of colors. Aluminum conducts heat freely. To avoid heat-loss and condensation problems, install only aluminum windows built with a thermal break, unless you live in a warm climate. A thermal break, usually a plastic or rubber strip that insulates the outside of the frame from the inside, prevents the frame from conducting heat out and cold in.

Steel: Steel casement, awning, and hopper windows were once popular, but steel windows are seldom seen in residential construction today. You may find basement-window inserts of steel, but steel windows are mostly limited to industrial applications where they offer fire resistance.

Fiberglass and composites: Manufacturers are now incorporating fiber-reinforced resins and new composite materials in window frames. Tough Ultrex plastic cladding is available in some lines; manufacturers say it will stand up to weather, pollutants, and salt water. The fiber-reinforced cladding also strengthens the window frame.

GLASS

Much advancement in window technology centers on the glass itself, notably low-E (low-emissivity) glazing. A microscopically thin coating of metal oxides moderates heat transmission through low-E glass. The coating allows most solar radiation—visible light and heat—to pass through the glass while blocking long-wave radiation—the heat that radiates from surfaces. A double-glazed window of low-E glass can lower energy costs year-round.

In the winter, short-wavelength solar rays pass through the low-E coating, bringing light and heat into a room. The solar energy heats the floor, walls, furniture, and other objects,

DOUBLE-HUNG WINDOW

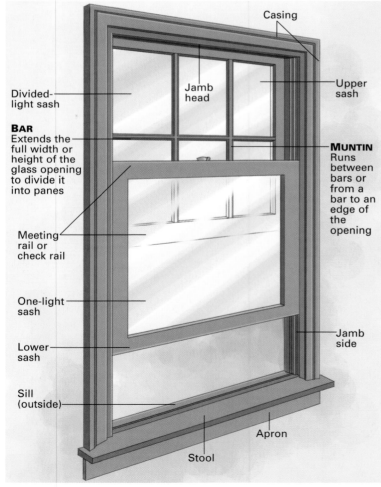

Casing

Jamb head

Upper sash

Divided-light sash

BAR
Extends the full width or height of the glass opening to divide it into panes

MUNTIN
Runs between bars or from a bar to an edge of the opening

Meeting rail or check rail

One-light sash

Lower sash

Jamb side

Sill (outside)

Apron

Stool

which then radiate long-wave heat rays. Low-E glass reflects these long radiant-heat waves, along with heat from the home's heating system, back into the room, reducing heat loss.

During the summer, low-E glass reflects the long-wave heat that radiates from sidewalks, driveways, and other buildings instead of letting it into the house. This reduces the heat gain inside, which lowers the cost of keeping the home cool.

Manufacturers also claim that low-E glass blocks some fade-causing ultraviolet (UV) radiation. Low-E glass can affect the color balance of light coming through, too, so look for neutral color transmission.

The U-factor indicates how well a window insulates against heat passage: A lower U-factor indicates greater insulating qualities. In some windows, an inert gas such as argon replaces the air between the panes to improve insulation. (Gas-filled windows may not be suitable for high-altitude locations.) A coated polyester film between the panes reduces the U-factor in other windows. Even the pane separators around the edge of the window contribute: Windows with wood or plastic ones—so-called warm-edge windows— insulate better.

Look for a National Fenestration Rating Council (NFRC) label, which lists a window's U-factor and other efficiency ratings. The American Architectural Manufacturers Association (AAMA) and Window and Door Manufacturer's Association (WDMA) rate windows for air infiltration, water resistance, and other performance qualities. Window dealers should be able to provide this information for their lines.

Comparing window features and attributes takes considerable time and patience. But it's important to find the windows with exactly the combination of features and performance qualities you want.

WINDOW CONSTRUCTION

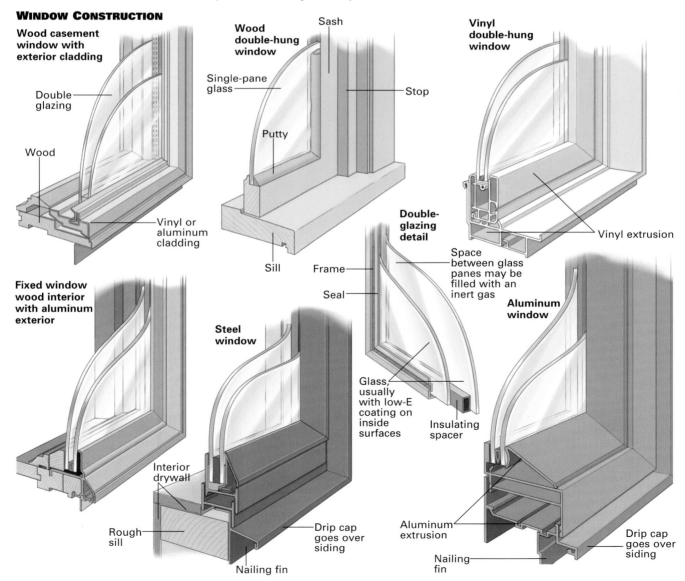

Wood casement window with exterior cladding
- Double glazing
- Wood
- Vinyl or aluminum cladding

Wood double-hung window
- Sash
- Single-pane glass
- Putty
- Stop
- Sill

Vinyl double-hung window
- Vinyl extrusion

Fixed window wood interior with aluminum exterior

Steel window
- Interior drywall
- Rough sill
- Drip cap goes over siding
- Nailing fin

Double-glazing detail
- Frame
- Seal
- Space between glass panes may be filled with an inert gas
- Glass, usually with low-E coating on inside surfaces
- Insulating spacer

Aluminum window
- Aluminum extrusion
- Nailing fin
- Drip cap goes over siding

REMOVING EXISTING WINDOWS

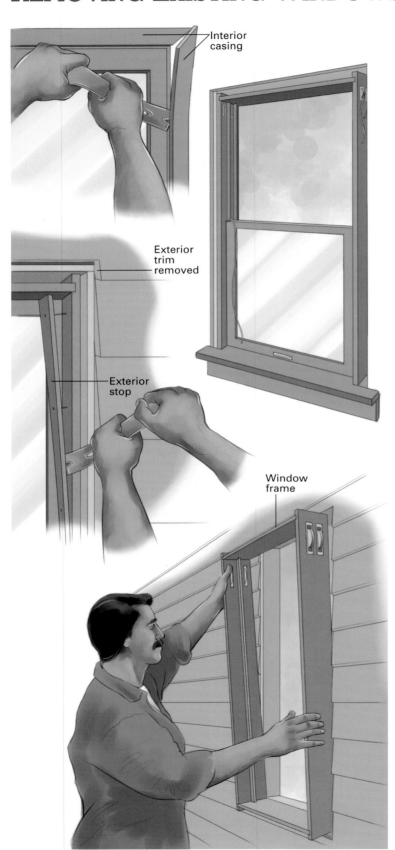

Interior casing

Exterior trim removed

Exterior stop

Window frame

You don't want to remove your old windows before you have the new ones, but you'll need exact measurements of the rough opening to order the new windows. To measure the rough opening easily, remove the inside casings all around the window. With the rough opening revealed, measure the width between the inner edges of the trimmer studs and the height from the top of the rough sill to the bottom of the header, as shown in the illustration at top left on page 60. The opening may not be square, so take several measurements. The new window must fit within the smallest dimensions.

REMOVING A WOOD-FRAMED WINDOW

You can remove a wood-framed window from inside or outside the house, whichever is most convenient. The steps here describe removal of a double-hung window, but the procedure for any wood-framed window would be similar. Work carefully to protect any wood trim that you want to reuse.

■ Start by removing the interior window trim. Carefully tap a broad, flat pry bar under one edge of the trim and gently pry it up. Don't pry it all the way at first; work your way slowly upward, raising it a little at a time to avoid breaking the trim. If any nails pull through the trim, remove them later with a claw hammer or pry bar.

■ To remove the inside sash, take off the inside stops—the narrow strips that form the channel for the sash—using a pry bar. Before you pull the sash out of the opening, disconnect the sash-weight cords. The knotted end of a cord usually fits into a hole in the side of the sash; you can disconnect them one at a time by tilting the edge of the sash out of the opening. Let each weight down gently. If there is a spring-loaded balance, twist the metal top to loosen it, then detach it from the sash.

■ You can remove the outside sash from inside, but it's easier to work outside, if possible. To remove the sash, first pry off the exterior trim. Then remove the exterior stops, and remove the sash the same way you did the inside one.

■ Take off the apron and the stool. Pry off the jambs, if possible. It is often easiest to drive the nails through the jambs and sill with a nail set, then lift out the window frame as a unit.

REMOVING A NAILING-FIN WINDOW

Almost all metal- or vinyl-framed windows are attached to the sheathing on the outside of the house with nails through a fin around the frame. Siding covers the fin; trim covers the gap between the siding and the window.

■ To remove a nailing-fin window, first pry off all the exterior trim. Work carefully so the trim can be reused. The nailing fin is usually about 1½ inches wide, so measure 1¾ inches out from the window frame all around. Mark the outline on the siding.

■ Install a flooring blade in your circular saw (you may hit some nails), and set the saw's cutting depth to ⅛ inch deeper than the thickness of the siding. Cut along the lines, saving the pieces of siding.

■ Carefully pry the nails from the fin and lift out the window.

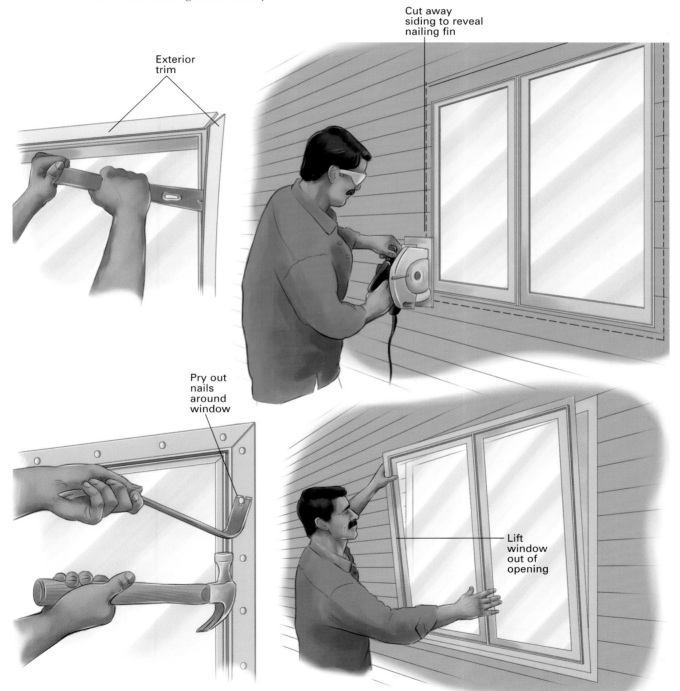

Cut away siding to reveal nailing fin

Exterior trim

Pry out nails around window

Lift window out of opening

STRUCTURAL PREPARATIONS

ALTERING AN EXISTING OPENING

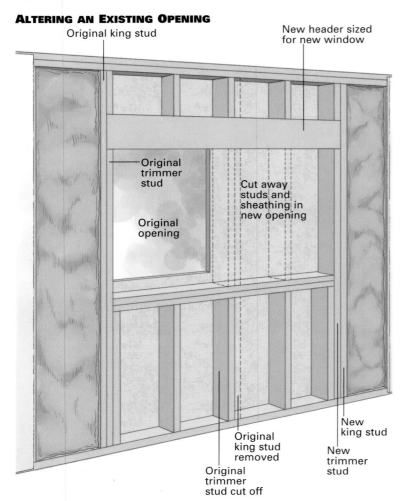

Original king stud

New header sized for new window

Original trimmer stud

Cut away studs and sheathing in new opening

Original opening

New king stud

Original king stud removed

New trimmer stud

Original trimmer stud cut off

NEW WINDOW OPENING IN PLATFORM FRAMING

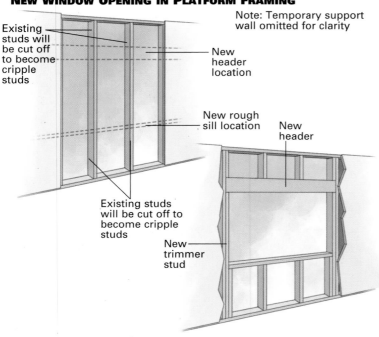

Existing studs will be cut off to become cripple studs

Note: Temporary support wall omitted for clarity

New header location

New rough sill location

New header

Existing studs will be cut off to become cripple studs

New trimmer stud

Installing windows requires framing alterations similar to those for doors. This section explains the differences between framing a window opening and framing a door opening. Before you begin, read the sections on framing (pages 12–17) and door installation (pages 20–29).

MAKING THE ROUGH OPENING

Even though a window opening requires additional framing members beneath the window, it is often simpler to make than a door opening. You don't have to install a floor-level sill and a threshold, for example. And you can probably avoid wiring or plumbing alterations because pipes and wires usually run below the window.

Here's how to frame a window opening in an existing wall:

■ First shore up the wall and remove the interior covering in the window area. Leave the wall's bottom plate intact.

■ Install the king studs, trimmer studs, and header, as shown in illustration at left.

■ Construct a rough sill from 2× material. It's good practice to double the sill on wide openings for rigidity. The double sill also provides more backing for nailing on window trim. In some parts of the country, double sills are routinely installed for all windows, and they may be required by local building codes.

■ Position the rough sill in the opening. Level it, and cut cripple studs to support it. Toenail the cripple studs at the bottom; face-nail one cripple stud against the trimmer on each side.

LINING UP THE TRIM

Consider how the door and window trim on the same wall will line up horizontally, both inside and outside the house. It can be difficult to make a continuous line across the tops, especially if you are trying to match existing windows and doors. The height of door and window head jambs varies among manufacturers, so if you align the upper edges of the head trim, the openings themselves may not line up.

You may be able to balance elements to solve this problem. For instance, if two windows flank a door, set them so their tops line up, leaving the top of the door trim at a different height. Each situation will require its own solution.

FLASHING THE OPENING

Flashing paper

Overlap corners

Hammer stapler

Apply bead of caulk on both sides and bottom just before setting a nailing-fin window in place. Caulk top also for a window with nail-through trim

LEVELING THE WINDOW
(Nailing-fin window shown)

Carpenter's level

Flashing paper overlaps nailing fin at top of window

Shim

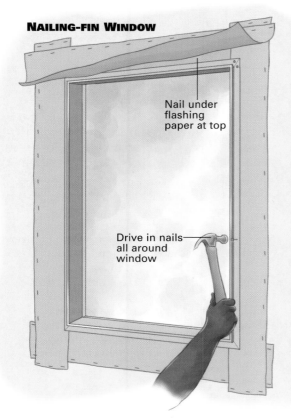

NAILING-FIN WINDOW

Nail under flashing paper at top

Drive in nails all around window

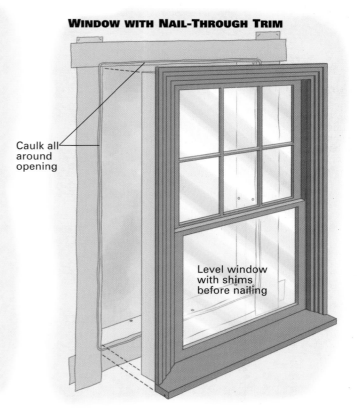

WINDOW WITH NAIL-THROUGH TRIM

Caulk all around opening

Level window with shims before nailing

INSTALLING THE WINDOW

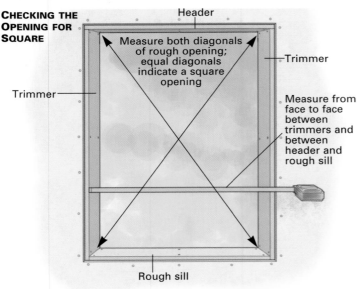

CHECKING THE OPENING FOR SQUARE

Header

Trimmer

Trimmer

Measure both diagonals of rough opening; equal diagonals indicate a square opening

Measure from face to face between trimmers and between header and rough sill

Rough sill

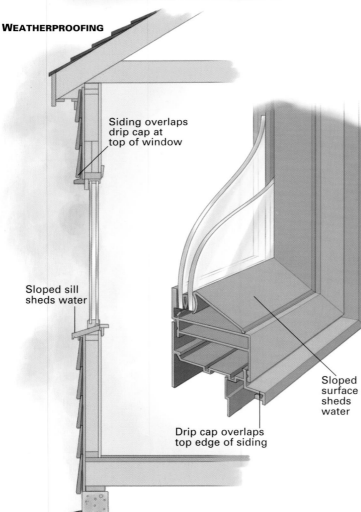

WEATHERPROOFING

Siding overlaps drip cap at top of window

Sloped sill sheds water

Sloped surface sheds water

Drip cap overlaps top edge of siding

Old-fashioned wood windows were tedious to install. It took lots of shimming and trimming to get that perfect fit. Today's windows are considerably faster and easier to install.

WINDOW FLASHING

Like doors, windows are generally installed by nailing through either the trim or nailing fins. Before you start, make sure that the opening is square, as shown at left.

Check the manufacturer's directions for flashing the window. Some windows don't require additional flashing because of the design of the frame and nailing fins. Otherwise a Z-flashing is usually required. The cross-section illustration at left shows how the metal Z-flashing tucks under the housewrap or underlayment, over the top of the wood trim, and down over the front face of the trim. Installing the flashing this way prevents water from running down the wall and getting behind the siding at the window head jamb. As a general rule, flashings and layers of building materials should always overlap so that water flows down the front surfaces without getting to the back.

Since the thickness of exterior window trim can vary, the Z-flashing is often custom-made for the top of a window. The flashings are easy to make from galvanized steel or aluminum flashing metal. To form sharp, straight bends in the metal for the Z-flashing, clamp it between two pieces of straight wood, placing the bending line along the top edge of the wood. Then working back and forth along its length, fold the metal at a right angle. Aluminum is easier to bend this way than galvanized steel.

INSTALLING A STANDARD WINDOW

■ Set the window in the rough opening. Have someone help position the window and hold it in place.

If a window is awkwardly heavy or large, you may be able to remove the operable sash to lighten it somewhat and give a place to hang on to it. Be careful not to scratch the glass or the frame when handling the window.

To position a window high on a wall, rent a scaffold for the installation; don't assume you will be able to do it from a ladder. If you know you will be installing a window high on a wall or in a place that's difficult to reach from outside, ask the dealer about windows with folding nailing fins. These fins lie flat against the unit so you can set the window in the opening inside the house and slide it outward on the rough sill. The fins then snap open, then you nail the window into the opening from the outside.

■ Center the window from side to side in the opening. Tack one of the upper corners in place, but don't drive the nail all the way in.

■ Level the sill. Check the manufacturer's instructions to see whether shimming is recommended at this point. Tack the lower corner diagonally opposite the upper corner that you tacked first.

■ Ensure that the window is square and operates smoothly and that the operable sashes sit evenly in their openings.

■ Tack the other two corners. Shim the unit if recommended. Install shims carefully: Too

little shimming may allow parts of the unit to sag; too much may bow the jambs. Either way, the window may stick or jam.

■ When you're sure that everything is properly adjusted, drive in the nails.

■ Install exterior flashings, as required. Caulk around the exterior after the siding is installed. Remember to insulate the spaces around the window, following the manufacturer's recommendations.

■ Install the hardware. Unlike doors, windows usually come with all of the necessary hardware, including locks. The window unit often comes with most of the hardware already installed.

INSTALLING A GREENHOUSE WINDOW

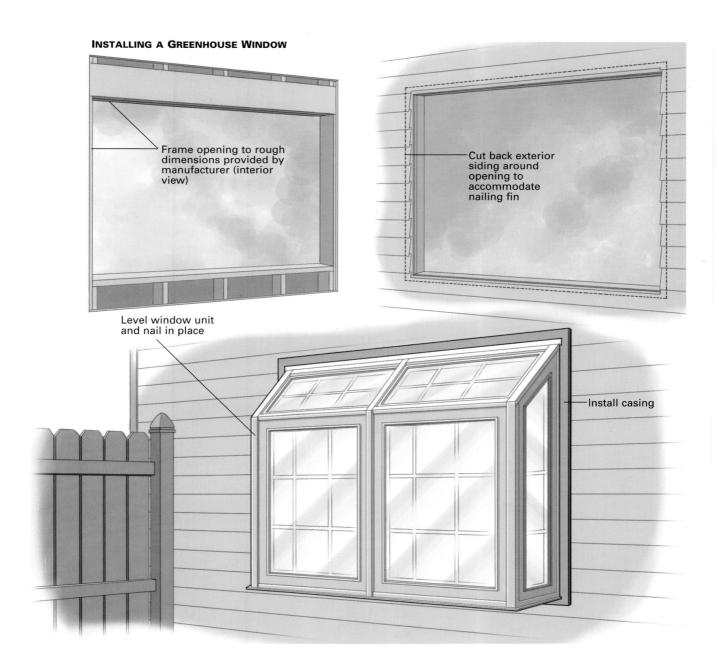

Frame opening to rough dimensions provided by manufacturer (interior view)

Cut back exterior siding around opening to accommodate nailing fin

Level window unit and nail in place

Install casing

BAY WINDOWS

You can buy a bay window (or a bow window) ready-made in a standard size, in a kit that you assemble, or buy one custom-made to your specifications. The window can be installed in two ways: by fitting it into a standard window opening or by altering the wall beneath the opening to create a bay.

The latter method involves more construction but creates an alcove that adds a little space and a lot of charm to the room. Unless the window fits against a soffit, it will need a roof.

If you buy a ready-made unit or a kit, ask the dealer whether the unit includes a precut roof—many do.

SUPPORTING A BAY WINDOW

Fender washer

Drive screw through sheathing into stud

Cut away siding for roof installation

Plumber's tape

Plywood roof section

Hip rafter

Insulation

INSTALLING A ROOF ON A BAY WINDOW

Step flashing

Flashing

Roofing

Drip edge

INSTALLING A BAY WINDOW IN A STANDARD OPENING

A wood- or metal-framed bay window installs in much the same way as a standard window. Some bay windows fit against the existing siding, others mount to the wall sheathing; be sure to read and follow the manufacturer's directions when you prepare the wall for the window installation.

■ Have two or three people help you set the window into the opening from the outside, and hold it or brace it in position.

■ From the inside, place a carpenter's level on the stool (the interior windowsill), and slip shim shingles between the window and the rough sill to level it. When the window is level, nail the stool to the rough sill through the shims.

■ Check for plumb on both sides of the window with a level. Shim the sides to make any adjustments and to achieve a sung fit. On wood-framed windows, nail the sides through the shims to the trimmer studs on either side. On metal-framed windows, nail the flanges to the exterior of the house.

■ Shim between the headboard and the header, and drive in nails.

■ Some bay windows call for knee braces underneath; check the instructions for your window. If they are required and the manufacturer didn't supply them, make them from 2×4s or decoratively cut 2×12s. Attach them to the house with lag screws driven into studs. Fasten the top of the knee brace to the bottom of the window with wood screws. Metal-framed bay windows generally do not need braces.

INSTALLING A PRECUT BAY WINDOW ROOF

■ Remove wooden drip cap around the top of the bay window. Fit the front and sides of the roof together on top of the window and mark the outline of the roof on the house siding.

■ Set the cutting depth on your circular saw to slightly more than the thickness of the siding. (Install a flooring blade on the saw; you'll probably run into some nails when you make this cut.) Cut along the lines, then remove the siding.

■ Fit the roof together against the side of the house and mark the outline on the underlayment beneath the siding. (If there is none, staple 15-pound felt to the sheathing inside the opening.) Measure the thickness of

the plywood roof sections and snap new chalk lines that distance inside the roof outline. The end rafter, hip rafters, and common rafters will be installed so that the top edges fall along these inner lines.

■ Tie the top of the window to the house with plumber's tape—perforated metal strapping sold in hardware stores. Using long screws with washers, attach the metal to the top of the window frame and the wall, driving the screw into a stud in the wall.

■ Nail the rafters in place, starting with the two hip rafters. These are beveled along the top outer edge so that the roof panels will lie solidly against them.

■ Lay a length of insulation over the top of the window with the foil face down. Put the roof panels in place and nail them to the rafters. Nail metal drip edges along the roof surface at the eaves. Cover the roof with 15-pound felt. Overlap the hips, and staple.

■ Shingle the roof to match the house, installing flashing between the roof and the wall as you work. Step flashing is used where the roof slopes down on each side, and a single length of metal flashing is used across the top. The same method works for all types of roofs.

You can cut aluminum pieces 10 inches long and as wide as the exposure of the shingles for step flashing. (The exposure is the distance from the butt of one shingle to the butt of the next one up, usually 5 inches for wood and composition shingles and 7 inches for shakes.) Precut step flashing shingles are also available.

The illustration on the opposite page shows how the first piece of flashing slips under the siding and lies under the doubled first row of shingles. The next piece of flashing slips under the siding and is covered by the second row of shingles and so on up the side. Flash both sides in this manner as you shingle the roof. Next apply the hip shingles.

The final step is to apply the strip flashing across the top. To do this, cut a length of flashing 6 to 8 inches wide and as long as the roof plus 6 inches. Bend 3-inch ears on each end, then bend the flashing lengthwise in the middle and slip one leg of the angle under the siding. Spread roofing cement on the top row of shingles under the flashing, and press the flashing into it. Coat the underside of the ears with roofing cement and bend them over the hip shingles. Finally, run a bead of caulk along the gap between the siding and the shingles.

BAY WINDOWS
continued

ADDING JOISTS TO SUPPORT AN ALCOVE

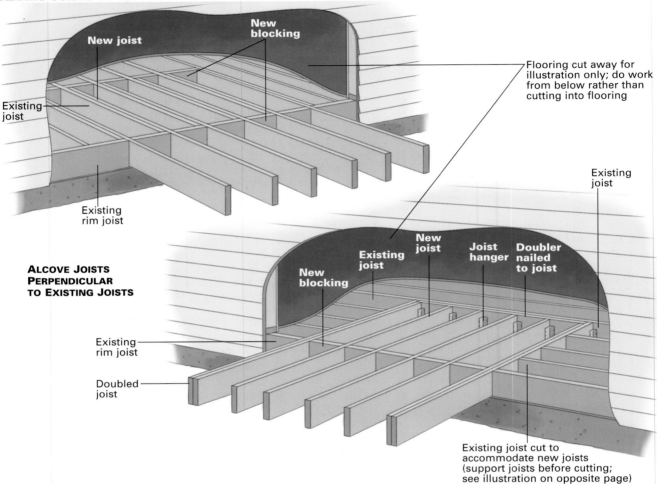

New joist

New blocking

Flooring cut away for illustration only; do work from below rather than cutting into flooring

Existing joist

Existing rim joist

Existing joist

ALCOVE JOISTS PERPENDICULAR TO EXISTING JOISTS

New blocking

Existing joist

New joist

Joist hanger

Doubler nailed to joist

Existing rim joist

Doubled joist

Existing joist cut to accommodate new joists (support joists before cutting; see illustration on opposite page)

BUILDING AN ALCOVE FOR A BAY WINDOW

Altering the house wall and floor to create an alcove that conforms to the bay window is more complex than simply placing a bay window in an opening. However, the new look and added utility for the room are worth the effort. The bay can be a snug spot for reading or perhaps a breakfast nook.

■ Begin by framing the opening as you would for a door. The rough opening will need to be larger than it would be for a window in a flat wall; check the manufacturer's instructions for the rough dimensions.

■ Extend the floor beyond the house wall to support the alcove. Build the floor on cantilevered joists the same size as the existing ones, extending out from the wall above the foundation for a floating effect. before you start work on the floor, shore up the existing floor from beneath, following the procedures shown on the facing page.

INSTALLING CANTILEVERED JOISTS

Let the support joists reach under the existing floor a distance equal to at least twice the depth of the alcove overhang. (If the bay window extends 2 feet, the new joists should reach at least 4 feet back under the house.) The direction the existing joists run in relation to the direction of the new joists determines how you install the new ones.

PARALLEL JOISTS: When the existing floor joists run the same direction the cantilevered joists will, just nail each new joist to the side of an existing one, as shown in the illustration at top left.

PERPENDICULAR JOISTS: When the existing floor joists run at right angles to the alcove joists, sections of several floor joists must be removed. Here's how to do that:

■ Determine how many of the existing joists must be cut out to make room for the new joists. Snap chalk lines along the bottoms of the joists to be cut, making the marks 3 inches wider than the actual opening on each side to allow for a doubled joist on each side.

■ Shore up the existing floor on both sides of the area where you'll remove joists. To do this, place supports beneath the joists to be cut, 2 feet back from the planned cut on each side. Build the temporary support system as shown at right below with 4×4 beams wedged tightly in place and toenailed together. Toenail the beams to the floor joists.

■ The full-length joist just beyond the cut ones will then support the ends of the alcove joists. Reinforce it by nailing another joist of the same size to the back of it. The reinforcing joist must be supported at both ends, so make it as long as the existing one. Wedge the reinforcing joist in place on the backside of the existing joist. Then nail it to the existing joist.

■ Cut out the marked sections of the joists with a saber saw or a reciprocating saw. Cut as far as you can with the power tools, then finish the cuts with a handsaw. Pry the joists loose from the subfloor, and cut the nails flush with end-cutting pliers.

■ Remove a portion of the rim joist where the joists will extend out from the house. Drill holes for the blade at each end of the section to be removed. Insert the saw blade in a start hole, and cut away the rim joist.

■ Cut the alcove joists, allowing about 6 inches of extra length on each one. To install the alcove joists, place one support joist at each side of the opening and nail it to the ends of the cut floor joists. Facenail a second joist to the first one to make a double joist. Hang the intervening joists, spacing them the same as the existing floor joists— usually 16 inches on center. Nail joist hangers to the reinforced existing joist to support the inner end of the alcove joists. After you finish installing the new joists, cut blocking to fit between them at the top of the foundation to replace the missing sections of the rim joist. Remove the support system.

BUILDING THE ALCOVE BASE

SUPPORTING PERPENDICULAR JOISTS FOR CUTTING

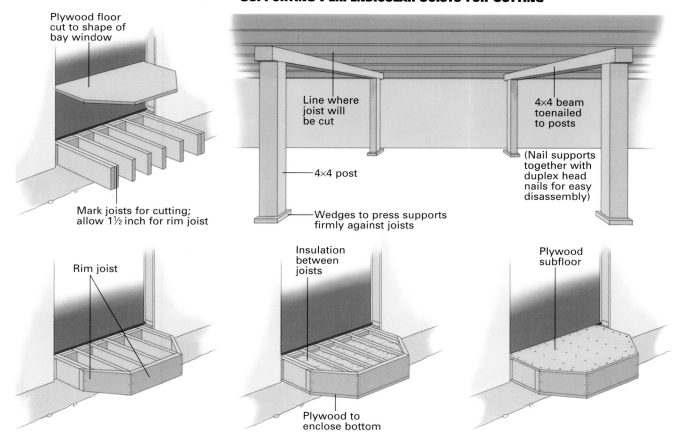

Plywood floor cut to shape of bay window

Mark joists for cutting; allow 1½ inch for rim joist

Line where joist will be cut

4×4 post

Wedges to press supports firmly against joists

4×4 beam toenailed to posts

(Nail supports together with duplex head nails for easy disassembly)

Rim joist

Insulation between joists

Plywood to enclose bottom

Plywood subfloor

TRIMMING THE WINDOW

There are several ways to trim the exterior and interior of a window. Refer to the section on trimming doors (pages 30–31) before you begin.

EXTERIOR TRIM

Window trim has a decorative aspect, but it serves a function, too: It keeps the weather out of the joint between the window and the siding. Traditionally, window trim was made from boards, called casing, applied to the sides, top, and bottom of a window, forming a frame or border around the window.

Some new windows don't need trim for weather protection. Aluminum and vinyl windows and others that have nailing fins and windows with preinstalled casing can all be finished by bringing the siding up to them.

Windows with nailing fins tend to look more contemporary when left untrimmed, but trim can be installed if the design of a home requires it. For the trim to lay flat against the house, you may have to rabbet the back of the trim piece to clear the nailing fins. Windows that come with preinstalled casings can sometimes be ordered with special trim widths or styles.

Options for exterior trim are:
■ Place trim of the same width around all four sides of the window, like a picture frame.

■ Install a sill at the bottom of the window, and trim the sides and top with same-width boards. Another board—an apron—sometimes goes below the sill.

The second style gives a traditional look. The picture-frame trim style is often chosen for nailing-fin windows and other nonwood windows without sills.

INSTALLING EXTERIOR TRIM

■ Measure for the casing with a steel tape measure. When the sill protrudes from the wall and extends beyond the side casings, measure the side casings first.
■ With the tip of the tape measure on the windowsill, extend the tape vertically along the side jamb just past the point where it intersects with the head jamb. This distance plus ¼ inch equals the length of the side casings for butt-joined trim. This allows for a ¼-inch reveal, or set back, from the edge of the jamb when the casing is installed.
■ Bevel the casings on the bottom to match the sill slope, then cut the casings to length. Tack them in place, then determine the length of the head casing by measuring the distance between the outside edges of the side casings. With butt-joined trim, the usual practice is to add ½ inch to the length to allow the head casing to extend ¼ inch beyond each side casing.

NEW WINDOWS CAN MATCH ARCHITECTURAL STYLES

It used to be that if you wanted Craftsman-style windows or some other particular look to match existing windows or to suit an architectural style, you had to scour salvage yards or have windows custom made, at great expense. Today's savvy manufacturers have re-created many classic styles from Gothic to Craftsman in special lines of designer and architectural windows, as shown at right and at left on the opposite page. In some window lines, removable grills can change the window to match any style, as shown at center and right on the opposite page.

MEASURING FOR WINDOW TRIM

Bevel-cut bottom
end of casing side
to match sill slope

FOR STUCCO OR SHINGLE SIDING
(Miter-joined trim)

Measure inside-to-inside
distance between side
casings to determine
length of head casing
between miter cuts

¼-inch
reveal
at top
and
sides

Sill

FOR WOOD SIDING
(Butt-joined trim)

Side
jamb

Head
jamb

Measure from
sill to head
jamb, then
add ¼ inch
for length of
side casings

¼-inch
reveal
at top
and
sides

Measure to outside
of side casings to
determine length
of head casing

Sill

FOR WINDOWS WITHOUT SILLS

Install bottom casing first,
then measure side casings
as on a window with a sill

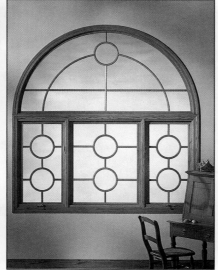

TRIMMING THE WINDOW
continued

Casings installed over wood siding are cut square on the top. If the trim is being installed on stucco or shingle siding, the side and head casings are usually mitered where they intersect. In this case, the measurement for the head casing is taken between the inside edges of the side casings, and the miter is cut from that dimension.

■ For a bottom casing on a window without a sill, determine the length by measuring between the inside edges of the window's side jambs and adding twice the width of the side casing plus ½ inch for the reveal and another ½ inch for overhang. Tack this piece in position, allowing ¼ inch of bottom-jamb reveal. Then determine the lengths of the side casings by measuring from the top edge of the bottom casing to ¼ inch past the bottom side of the head jamb. Once these side casings are tacked into position, the head casing can be measured, cut, and installed as described for trimming windows with sills.

WINDOWS WITH NAILING FLANGES

Metal windows and other types with nailing flanges should be installed before the siding. Casing may or may not be necessary.

■ Shingles: Casing is optional. If you elect to install it, do so before applying the shingles.

■ Horizontal and vertical board siding and plywood: Casing is installed after siding.

■ Stucco, brick, and stone: No casing is used.

BUTT-JOINED WINDOW TRIM

Head casing

Side casing

Bevel-cut bottom of side casing to match sill slope

MITERED WINDOW TRIM

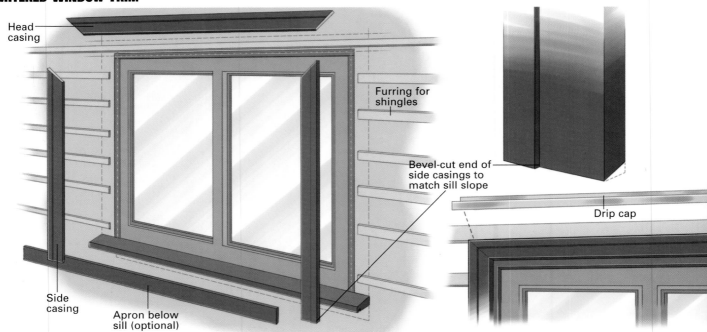

Head casing

Side casing

Apron below sill (optional)

Furring for shingles

Bevel-cut end of side casings to match sill slope

Drip cap

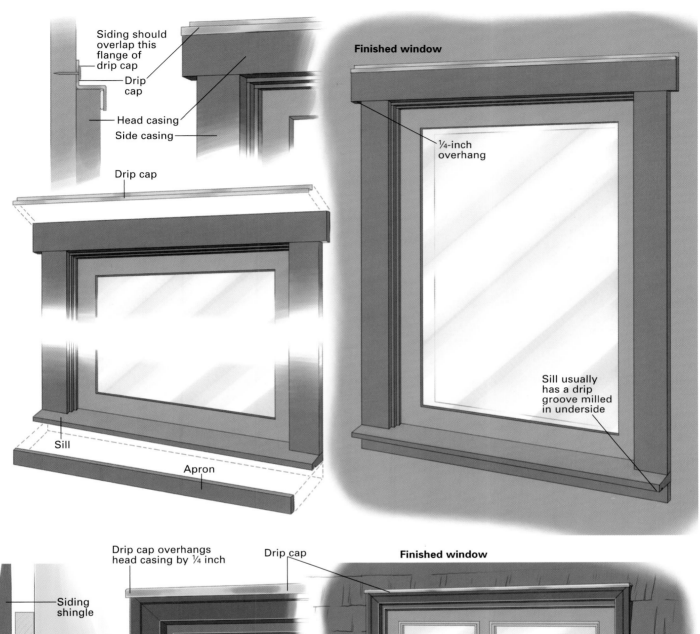

Siding should overlap this flange of drip cap

Drip cap

Head casing

Side casing

Drip cap

Finished window

¼-inch overhang

Sill usually has a drip groove milled in underside

Sill

Apron

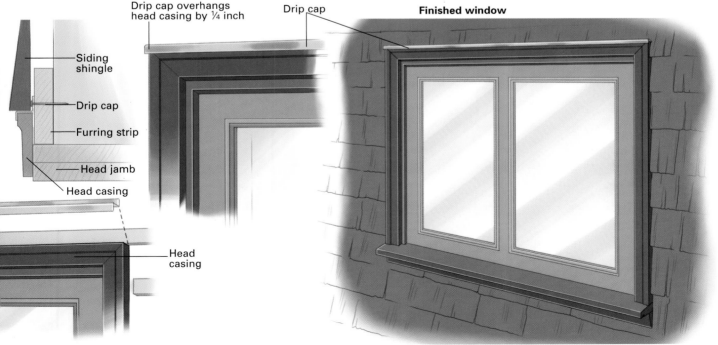

Drip cap overhangs head casing by ¼ inch

Drip cap

Finished window

Siding shingle

Drip cap

Furring strip

Head jamb

Head casing

Head casing

TRIMMING THE WINDOW
continued

TRIMMING A NAILING-FIN WINDOW

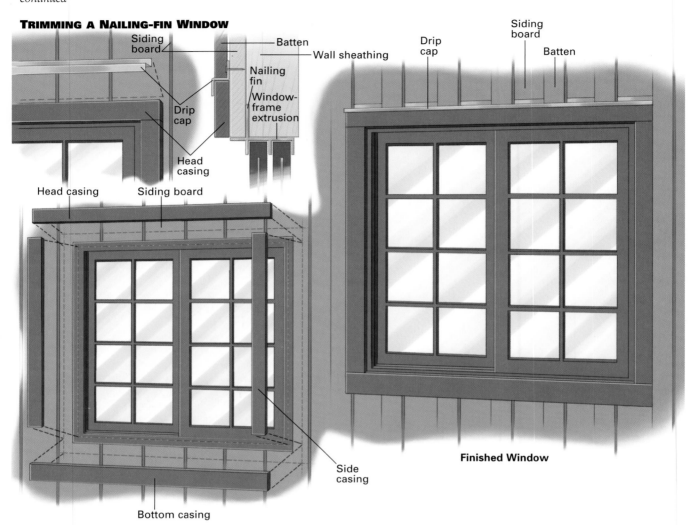

Siding board
Batten
Wall sheathing
Nailing fin
Window-frame extrusion
Drip cap
Head casing
Head casing
Siding board
Side casing
Bottom casing

Drip cap
Siding board
Batten

Finished Window

WOOD-FRAMED WINDOWS

Casing for wood-framed windows is installed before or after the siding, depending on the type of wall covering used.

■ Shingle, stucco, brick, and stone: Casing is usually installed before siding.

■ Horizontal or vertical board siding: Casing can be installed before or after siding.

■ Plywood siding: Casing is usually installed after siding.

If your house has a unique design that calls for unusual windows, wall coverings, or casing procedures, ask your window dealer to help you determine whether, when, and how to install casing.

CAULKING

If the casings will be painted, small gaps or cracks can be caulked first. Casings that will be stained or sealed with a clear material must fit together well or caulks will show through and be unsightly. A limited range of colored caulks is available, and one of these may match the stain of sealed wood.

NAILING

Hot-dipped galvanized common, box, and casing nails are most often used for exterior trim applications. They're weather-resistant and hold well. Finishing nails are not usually used on exteriors because they don't hold as well as the others.

Stainless-steel nails, though expensive, are the best choice if a clear finish is to be applied or if the nailheads will be exposed.

As a rule, nails should be evenly spaced, between 12 and 18 inches apart. The top and bottom nails should be about 1 inch from the ends of the casing. Closer nailing might be necessary where the stock is bowed or otherwise irregular.

INTERIOR TRIM OPTIONS

Mitered corner

Mitered Casing
(Picture-frame style)

Rounded corner

Drywall or plaster

No Casing

Mitered corner

Stool

Mitered Casing with Stool

Corner block

Butt joint

Block Casing

Butt joint

Apron

Butted Casing with Stool

Square corner

Drywall or plaster

Stool

Horn

No Casing with Stool

TRIMMING THE WINDOW
continued

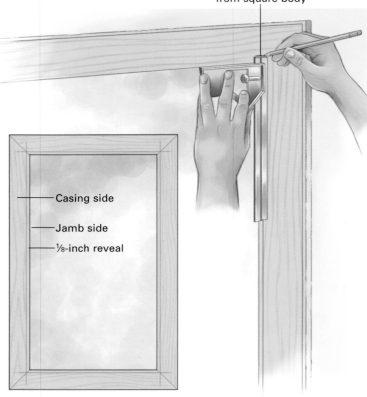

Blade extends ⅛ inch
from square body

Casing side

Jamb side

⅛-inch reveal

The interior casing sits back from the edge of the window jamb. This distance—the reveal—is usually ⅛ inch all around the window. You can mark the reveal easily on the edge of the jamb members with a pencil and combination square, as shown above.

Traditional interior window trim includes a stool—the inside windowsill—an apron, and casing along the two sides and across the top. This is still a popular way to finish an interior window, although windows can also be trimmed in the picture-frame style.

Although walls are generally of a standard thickness, you may encounter walls that aren't, particularly in an old house or one that has been remodeled. Windows manufactured to fit standard walls will require extensions on the inside jambs to bring them flush with the wall surface so casings can be installed. Some manufacturers will provide jamb extensions for their windows, but you will probably have to make them yourself. It's easy to do: Just plane material to the thickness of the window jamb, then ripsaw it to a width equal to the distance from the jamb edge to the wall surface. Glue and nail them to the jamb.

You can trim the side jambs of metal and vinyl windows entirely in wood, but more often these windows are installed with wallboard returns on the top and side jambs and a wood stool and apron. This is an attractive and functional arrangement. Wallboard stools are sometimes installed, but these do not wear very well.

Before you start, check for jamb flaws and correct them. Look for jambs that protrude beyond the plane of the wall. These make it difficult to make good corner joints. Planing will usually solve the problem. Also look for jambs that don't quite meet the surface of the finish wall. Fix these by installing jamb extensions to bring the surfaces even or planing down the wallboard. A bowed or curved jamb usually can be corrected by straightening the jamb as you drive in the trim nails.

Finally, remember to use finishing nails that are appropriate for the thickness of the casing. For example, the most common casing—pine beveled—which is ⅜ inch thick and between 1⅝ and 2¼ inches wide—calls for 3d finishing nails at the jamb edge and 6d finishing nails at the trimmer edge. For the more traditional straight casing, which is usually Douglas fir stock 3½ inches wide and ¾ inch thick, use 6d finishing nails at the jamb edge and 8d finishing nails at the trimmer edge.

Window sashes and trim match the surrounding woodwork in this kitchen. White-painted jambs match the walls and break up the mass of stained wood.

STOOL INSTALLATION

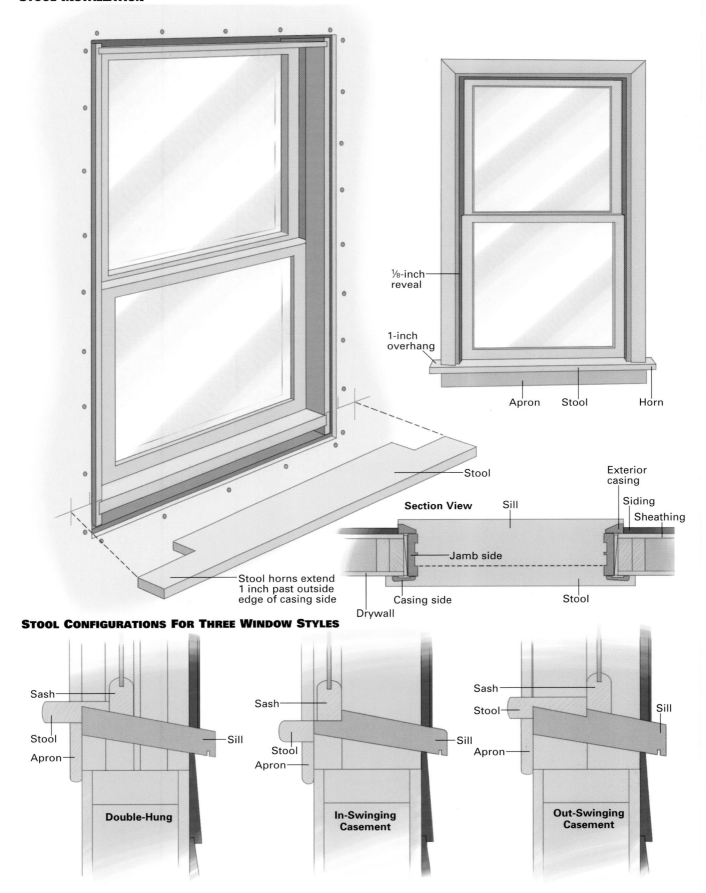

⅛-inch reveal

1-inch overhang

Apron Stool Horn

Stool

Stool horns extend 1 inch past outside edge of casing side

Exterior casing

Siding

Sheathing

Section View Sill

Jamb side

Casing side

Drywall

Stool

STOOL CONFIGURATIONS FOR THREE WINDOW STYLES

Sash

Stool

Apron

Sill

Double-Hung

Sash

Stool

Apron

Sill

In-Swinging Casement

Sash

Stool

Apron

Sill

Out-Swinging Casement

WINDOW TROUBLESHOOTING

Window problems range from sticking sashes to broken glass. Yet you can most often solve the problems with a little know-how and time, and save money and trouble in the long run.

BROKEN GLASS

If one pane of a double-glazed window is broken or cracked or if the seal between the panes has failed, indicated by fogging between the panes, the entire sash must be replaced.

WOOD-SASH WINDOW:

■ To replace a broken single pane in a wood-framed sash window, first remove the broken shards. (Wear gloves to protect your hands.)

■ Scrape out the putty with a putty knife. Pull out all the glazier's points and then scrape and sand the old wood.

■ Coat the bare surface with a sealer or linseed oil, which will keep the wood from drawing the oil out of the new putty or glazing compound.

■ Measure the window carefully and have a new piece of glass cut at a glass shop. Have the new pane cut ⅛ inch smaller in both height and width than the window opening itself. If the window isn't square or rectangular, make a template of the opening to take to the glass shop.

■ Working from the outside, spread a ⅛-inch-thick layer of glazing compound on the edge of the opening. Insert the new pane. Press it into the opening to seat it, but don't press so hard that you squeeze out the glazing compound.

■ Still working from the outside, tap the glazier's points in place around the window. Space them about 6 inches apart. Drive them in halfway with a hammer and screwdriver.

■ Roll some glazing compound into a rope about ½ inch thick. Press it into place with your fingers, covering the glazier's points.

■ Using the putty knife, press the rope in farther and leave a smooth, beveled bead, moving from one corner to the other in one continuous stroke. The compound should extend to the outer edge of the sash and should extend as high as the edge of the stop on the inside of the glass.

■ Clean the glass. When the putty or compound is dry enough to touch without leaving a fingerprint, repaint it. Let the paint lap onto the glass by about 1/16 inch.

GLASS RETENTION METHODS

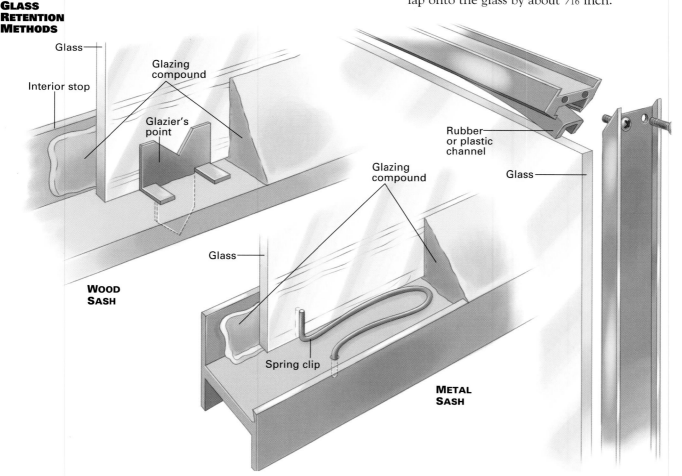

Glass

Interior stop

Glazing compound

Glazier's point

WOOD SASH

Glass

Glazing compound

Spring clip

METAL SASH

Rubber or plastic channel

Glass

FREEING A STUCK WINDOW

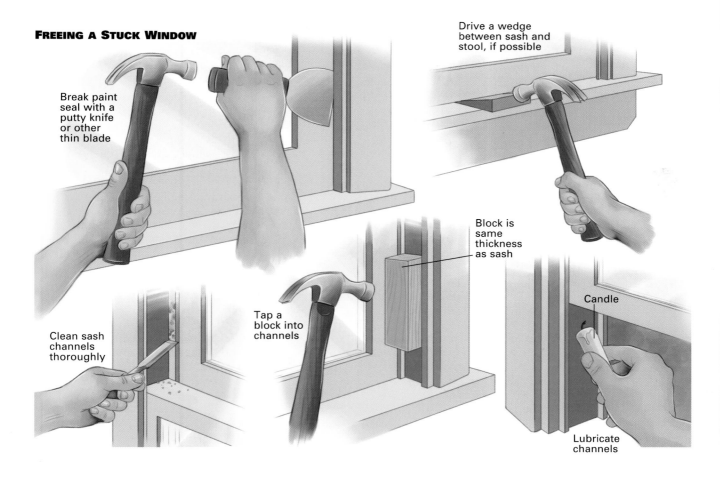

Break paint seal with a putty knife or other thin blade

Drive a wedge between sash and stool, if possible

Clean sash channels thoroughly

Tap a block into channels

Block is same thickness as sash

Candle

Lubricate channels

NONWOOD WINDOW: Casement window panes are replaced in much the same way as panes in wood-framed sash windows. However, spring clips hold the glass in place, instead of glazier's points. The clips usually fit into a hole in the window frame.

■ After removing the putty, sand the opening for the glass and repaint it to prevent corrosion. Replace the window pane as described above, using the clips instead of glazier's points.

■ Metal strips and a rubber gasket retain the panes in some casement windows. Make sure that the rubber gasket has not been damaged. If it has been, replace it.

■ To remove broken glass from aluminum sliding windows, the sash must be taken apart, usually by removing screws. The glass is held in place by a rubber gasket. Pull this out and remove all the broken glass. Reinstall the glass and gasket, then reassemble.

REPAIRING DAMAGED SCREENING

Screening in doors and windows dries and becomes brittle after a few seasons. Replace it when bumping it causes holes. New screen materials on the market offer increased resistance to tears and stretching. You can also buy conventional wire screening in sheets or in repair kits designed solely for fixing minor holes. Replace screening with the kind that's already in the frame.

■ If the screening is in a wood frame, first pry up the molding that holds the screen in place. Remove the screening and the staples. Cut new screen 1 inch larger than the opening and staple it in place, beginning with one staple at the top, stretching the screen taut and stapling the bottom. Then staple the sides in the same manner, working around the whole screen, tightening and stapling.

■ If the frame is aluminum, the screen is usually held in place by a rubber or plastic spline that presses into a recessed channel. Pry this beading out to remove the screen. To replace the screen, cut new screen about 1 inch larger than the opening, and press the screen into the channel, securing it with the beading. To make the job go faster and easier, buy the inexpensive tool for rolling the beading into place. Trim off the excess screen and spline with a utility knife or scissors.

WINDOW TROUBLESHOOTING
continued

UNSTICKING DOUBLE-HUNG WINDOWS

Who hasn't experienced the agony of a stuck window? Usually, it's the old double-hung style that gets stuck. It may have been painted shut or dirt or paint may have worked into the channels. Weather can also cause problems, as humidity swells the wood. Here are some tactics to try:

■ First try working your way around all the cracks with a putty knife—not a screwdriver, which would gouge the wood. Many hardware stores sell a small saw-like tool made to cut through paint-sealed joints.

■ If this doesn't loosen it up, try tapping a wedge between the bottom of the sash and the sill from the outside. Work slowly across the base of the window so that the sash moves upward evenly without binding.

■ If swollen wood is causing the window to bind, try cutting a 6-inch length of wood that fits snugly into the actual channel. Hammer it at various points, which should loosen the channel slightly, enabling the sash to move.

■ If none of this works, you'll have to remove the sash stops. Pry them out carefully so you can reuse them. With the stops out, remove the sashes and sand or plane both sides evenly until the window moves freely.

REPAIRING DOUBLE-HUNG WINDOWS

The mechanism of some double-hung windows can be modernized as well as repaired. Sash cords, which tend to break, can be replaced with chains or spring balances. Spring lifts can be adjusted to give the correct amount of tension.

REPLACING A SASH CORD:
■ Begin by removing the stop along the side that has the broken or twisted sash cord. It may be screwed in place. If not, loosen it with a chisel or a flat pry bar, working from one end, inside the channel, if possible, to minimize damage.

■ Once the stop molding for the lower sash has been removed, ease the sash out of the frame just enough to free the knotted end of the cord from the sash groove. Lower the weight gently and let the knot rest against the pulley.

■ To get at the weight, you might have to remove an access panel in the jamb side. If it has never been removed, it may be difficult to find under the paint. Search for the panel with a nail or awl, then find the one or two nails or screws that hold it in place. In very old houses, this panel may never have been cut completely through, and you will have to finish the job, using a drill and a keyhole saw. If there is no access panel, you will have to remove the window casing on that side to reach the weight.

If only the upper sash cord needs repair, you still must remove the lower sash. To remove the upper sash, slide it down as far as it will go and remove the parting stop between the two sashes.

If the parting stop is pressed into a groove, grip it with pliers to remove it. Put a protective piece of wood on each side of the parting strip so that it won't be damaged by the pliers. Remove the upper sash cord and weight in the same way as the lower ones.

■ Replace sash cords with chains, which require no maintenance and will last longer. Drop the chain down the channel and then run it through the hole at the top of the weight. Connect the weight to the chain with mechanic's wire.

■ Now put the sash back in place as if it were fully closed. For the lower window, raise the

SASH WEIGHTS

Protect parting stop during removal with wood strips or heavy cardboard

Pulley

Inner sash weight

Sash cord

Access panel (not on all windows)

Outer sash weight

Attach weight to chain with wire

Attach chain to sash with screw

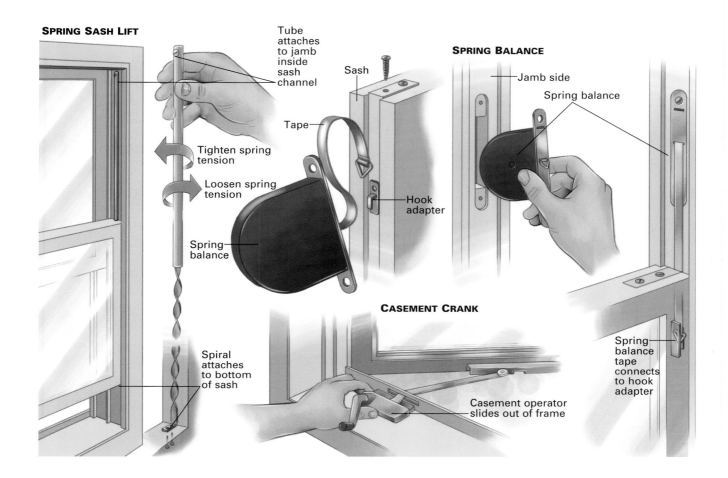

SPRING SASH LIFT

Tube attaches to jamb inside sash channel

Tighten spring tension

Loosen spring tension

Spring balance

Spiral attaches to bottom of sash

Sash

Tape

Hook adapter

SPRING BALANCE

Jamb side

Spring balance

CASEMENT CRANK

Casement operator slides out of frame

Spring balance tape connects to hook adapter

---

sash weight until it is just below the sash pulley. The upper window's weight should be about 2 inches from the bottom of the window opening. When you have adjusted the weight, fasten the chain securely to the sash by inserting two screws through the links. Make sure that the screw heads do not protrude from the slot.

■ Before you reinstall the panel cover and the stops, make sure that the window works smoothly.

ADJUSTING A SPRING LIFT: A spring lift looks like a metal tube that runs up the side of the window. It eliminates the need for sash cords and weights, and it can be tightened or loosened to adjust the movement of the window.

■ If the window tends to creep up after it has been opened, the spring is too tight. To loosen the spring, remove the tube at the top of the window and let the screw unwind two or three turns to the left. Keep the screw under control.

■ If the window does not move easily, give the screw a couple of turns to the right to increase tension.

REPLACING A SPRING BALANCE: This device can easily be installed to replace the sash cords and weight. Built something like a self-retracting steel measuring tape, it is designed to fit into the opening for the pulleys on a double-hung window frame. The tape hooks to an adapter screwed to the sash. Sash balances come in different sizes to fit different windows.

REPAIRING A CASEMENT WINDOW:

Most casement windows open with a crank. If the crank fails to open the window, first make sure the crank is secure on the operator shaft. It might have a setscrew or press onto splines.

■ If the crank is turning the shaft, check the gears in the operator mechanism. To do this, remove the handle. Then remove the screws holding the gear box to the side of the window frame. Finally, remove the arm by sliding it along the slot in the bottom of the sash until it lifts free. Worn or broken gears will have to be replaced. Take the old mechanism to the hardware store to help get the right replacement.

SKYLIGHTS

A skylight is the best source for direct natural light. Once considered a luxury, today's products are affordable and available in a broad range of styles, from simple plastic bubbles to those with electrically driven openers and shading devices. Putting one in might seem like a daunting task, but with basic carpentry skills, the right tools, and clear instructions, you can ensure that your new skylight will not only be beautiful, but trouble-free.

Twin operable skylights admit morning light and evening breezes to this master suite, left, built in an attic. A light well from the skylight directs light into the living room, below.

FORM AND FUNCTION

STYLE

Skylights are ordinarily square or rectangular, with either wood or metal frames. Flat glazing in skylights can be glass or plastic; bubble-type skylights are always plastic. Skylights can be operable (capable of opening for ventilation) or fixed (nonopening). A variation—the roof window—is designed to be installed at eye level, often in a steeply pitched roof as part of an attic remodeling. Many skylights or roof windows are suitable for do-it-yourself installation.

Consider where you want to install the skylight. Keep the project as simple and hassle-free as possible by knowing what's in the ceiling before you start cutting.

You can buy complete skylight kits at specialty window showrooms or home centers. As always, it pays to comparison shop and ask questions about energy efficiency, frame materials, and the unit's track record: Has it been around for a while and proven itself, or is it a new, less time-tested design?

CHOOSING THE LOCATION

A light well leads to the skylight when there's space between the roof and the room ceiling.

Your home's structure may limit suitable locations for a skylight. When you have several choices, think about the kind of light you'll be letting in. On a roof slope facing south or west, the skylight will admit a lot of direct summer sun, which can increase room temperatures and fade rugs and furniture. Placing the unit on an east or north slope will give you just as much light but less direct sunshine. Awnings, special glass, and other options can help control the amount of light that enters a room.

Consider access too. A skylight should be placed so that you can reach it for cleaning without endangering yourself.

CONTROLLING HEAT, VENTILATION, AND LIGHT

To prevent excessive heat buildup, consider operable or ventilating skylights. These units, installed high in the house, cool the interior considerably by allowing hot air to escape, while letting breezes in. They essentially perform the same function as cupolas in old Victorian homes, but employ modern technology. Here are some other factors to take into account:

■ Consider the slope on which the skylight will be installed. Sunlight strikes the earth's surface at a low angle during the winter and at a high angle during the summer. Thus a skylight that is more nearly vertical will receive more direct sunlight in the winter, when heat gain is desirable, and less in the summer, when it is not.

■ Small skylights on the north slope of a roof may not need shades, but large skylights, or those exposed to bright sun, will probably need some form of light control. Many skylight and roof window manufacturers offer exterior and interior awnings or blinds for their products to control the entry of light.

TYPICAL LIGHT WELL CONFIGURATIONS

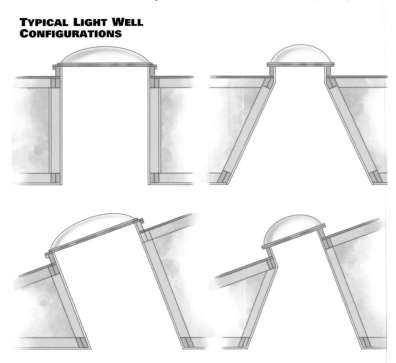

■ Glazing can also control light and UV radiation. Most of the glazing features discussed on pages 54 and 55 are available for skylights, including bronze- and gray-tinted glass, low-E reflective coatings, and gas-filled double-pane glazing. Plastic skylights are available with a bronze tint or a light-diffusing white frosted surface. Some manufacturers offer plastic glazing made of a honeycomb material specially designed to diffuse light evenly. The dead-air spaces in the honeycomb provide effective insulation.

■ If you want skylights to help heat the house in winter but keep it cool in summer, the answer might be low-E, argon-filled glazing, which lets in the sun's rays during the winter while keeping the heat from escaping. This can be combined with an awning or blind system that can be kept closed during the hot summer months.

Tubular skylights make maximum use of the sun's rays by reflecting and diffusing the light. Some, like the unit at left, are equipped with a light kit, turning the skylight into a ceiling light after the sun goes down.

LIGHT WELLS

If there is a ceiling below the roof where you want to install a skylight, you will need to construct a light well. This provides another way to control the quality of light entering the room. Light wells with straight shafts are easier to build than flared ones, but flaring the shaft will provide better light distribution and a more attractive appearance. (See Typical Light Well Configurations on the opposite page.)

The simplest installation is for a so-called cathedral window, which fits right into the roofline, as in many sunroom additions. This installation eliminates the need for a shaft.

The domed lens on top of this tubular skylight gathers and reflects light into the room. The tubular shaft has a reflective coating inside.

SECURITY AND SAFETY

If you use skylights or roof windows to convert an attic to a useable room, remember that building codes will require you to provide a minimum-sized window opening as an emergency exit if the room will be used for sleeping. As a rule, the exit window must be at least 24 inches high by 20 inches wide, with the sill not more than 44 inches from the floor. Check your local building code for current requirements in your area.

The local code may also specify what types of glazing are permissible in skylights. Laminated safety glass, tempered glass, or some combination of the two is usually required. There may also be some restrictions on plastic glazings, though these rarely apply to single-family houses. Finally, if you want to install a skylight on a part of the roof that is close to a property line, check to see whether any code restrictions apply. These restrictions are meant to help prevent the rapid spread of fire from house to house.

Roof windows are skylights that act as windows in a steeply pitched roof. They serve well when remodeling an attic to provide living space.

INSTALLING A SKYLIGHT

It isn't difficult to install a skylight, but the job must be done correctly and safely. This section discusses ways to frame the opening, install the skylight, and do a weather-tight job of flashing.

SAFETY FIRST

Start by reviewing the rules of safety. You'll be working on the roof, so wear shoes that grip well. Install safety lines to hang on to.

When you're working in the attic, keep your weight on the joists. Place boards or scraps of plywood temporarily across the joists to stand on.

And remember, cutting roof shingles and decking throws a tremendous amount of harmful dust around, and air in the attic contains dust and insulation fibers. So besides safety glasses and hearing protection, be sure that everyone wears a dust mask.

You can usually do your skylight work within a day, but check out the weather forecast for the next couple of days. Have a tarp with tie-downs ready to cover your roof opening if it rains.

INSTALLATION

Skylights and roof windows often come with all the necessary parts. These general instructions apply to installation of a curb-mount skylight using flashings fabricated separately. Always follow the manufacturer's instructions and recommendations.

CURB CONSTRUCTION

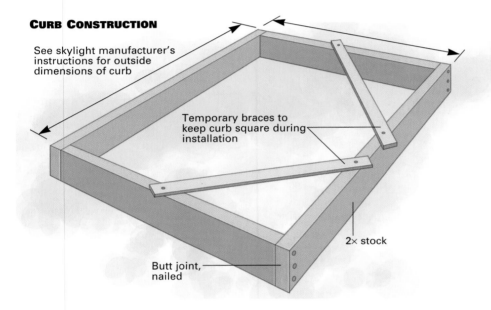

See skylight manufacturer's instructions for outside dimensions of curb

Temporary braces to keep curb square during installation

2× stock

Butt joint, nailed

TYPICAL SKYLIGHT FRAMING

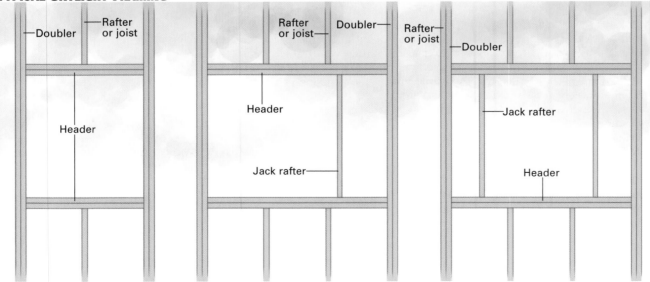

Doubler

Rafter or joist

Header

Rafter or joist

Doubler

Header

Jack rafter

Rafter or joist

Doubler

Jack rafter

Header

Units identified as self-flashing have the flashing incorporated into the skylight itself. These units are more likely to leak than conventional skylights; they are best installed by professional roofers. They're also difficult to install with thick roofing materials. But don't rule them out if you want a very low-profile skylight.

Installing a roof window is a lot like installing a wall window, and most of the work involves framing the opening in the roof. When the skylight is above a finished ceiling, you'll have additional framing for the ceiling opening and light well.

■ The first step is to build a curb for the skylight to rest on. The flashing will have to run up this curb on the sides; make sure the curb is about ¼ inch narrower than the head and base flashings so they will slip easily into place.

■ Build the curb from 2× lumber of appropriate width, as illustrated on the opposite page. Measure and cut carefully so that it is ⅜ inch smaller all around than the interior dimensions of the skylight. This gap allows the skylight to fit over both the curb and its step flashing.

When the curb is nailed together, square it with a framing square and by making sure the diagonal measurements are the same. Then tack two pieces of wood across the diagonal corners to hold it in shape.

LAYING OUT THE ROOF OPENING:

■ A skylight is normally positioned to center it or its light well in the ceiling of the room below. If there are no ceiling and light well, half of your construction problems are eliminated. If there is a ceiling, drive a nail up through it where you want the center of the light well to be.

■ In the attic, drop a plumb bob from the underside of the roof deck to the point of the nail in the ceiling to find the center of the roof opening. If necessary, move this point a few inches to eliminate unnecessary cutting of

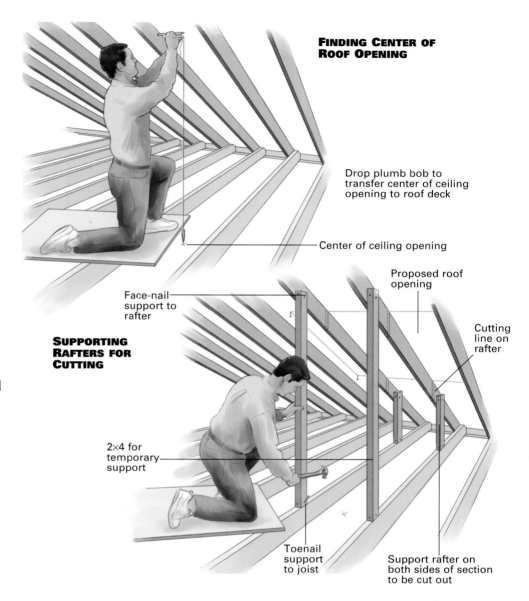

FINDING CENTER OF ROOF OPENING

Drop plumb bob to transfer center of ceiling opening to roof deck

Center of ceiling opening

SUPPORTING RAFTERS FOR CUTTING

Face-nail support to rafter

Proposed roof opening

Cutting line on rafter

2×4 for temporary support

Toenail support to joist

Support rafter on both sides of section to be cut out

rafters or joists. Try to line up one side of the skylight on an existing rafter.

The illustrations on the opposite page show some different methods for framing an opening. Choose the way that best meets your needs. The simplest way is to use existing rafters rather than building in one or more jack rafters.

■ Once you have found the center point of the roof opening, mark cutting lines for the inside dimensions of the curb across the rafters and the underside of the roof deck. Carefully measure this with a framing square. Drive a nail up through the roof at each corner mark.

■ Now measure down 3 inches below the bottom line of the curb outline (toward the eaves) and 3 inches above it (toward the ridge). Snap straight chalk lines across the bottoms of the rafters at these marks. The additional 3 inches above and below allows

INSTALLING A SKYLIGHT
continued

double headers to be installed between the rafters. The intervening rafters will be cut on these lines.

■ Before you cut, support the rafters by nailing 2×4s to them above and below the marks, with the bottom of the supports resting on ceiling joists. Toenail them in place. You can cut the opening in the roof now or wait until you've finished the interior framing.

When you cut it, have someone assist you with the cutout piece—it may be heavy.

CUTTING THE ROOF OPENING:

■ Working on the roof, snap chalk lines to connect all the nail points. The inside corners of the curb will be the points where the nails came through the roof.

■ The outside edge of the curb will be 1½ inches outside the nails. To give yourself a little room to work, snap another set of chalk lines 2 inches outside the original lines.

■ Set the cutting depth of a circular saw to the thickness of the roofing shingles and cut along the outermost lines. Use a disposable blade—you'll probably hit a lot of nails.

COMPLETED OPENING

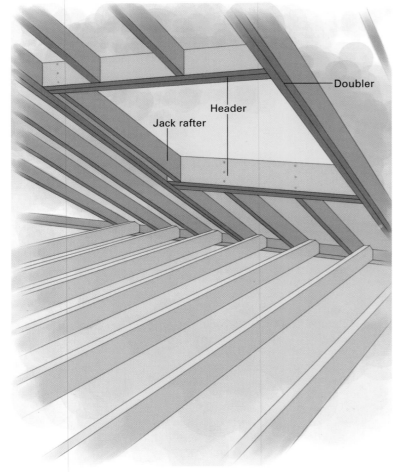

Doubler

Header

Jack rafter

■ Remove the shingles in the area. Snap new lines on the roof deck to mark the inside dimensions of the curb. (Use the nail holes as guides.)

■ Set the blade on the saw to cut ⅛ inch deeper than the thickness of the roof deck. Cut along the lines and remove the decking.

FRAMING THE OPENING:

■ Back inside the attic, cut away the rafters that cross the opening. Cut on the chalk lines you marked 3 inches above and below the outline of the curb.

■ At the top and bottom of the opening, measure the distance between the uncut rafters nearest each side of the opening. Cut four header boards of this length from stock the same size as the rafters.

■ Fit a header board at the top or bottom of the opening between the two existing uncut rafters. Nail through the rafters into the ends of the header with 16d nails. Nail through the header into the end of any cut rafter. Do the same at the other end of the opening.

■ Now nail the second header board in place against the first at each end of the opening.

■ Install jack rafters as needed. Remove the temporary braces.

SELECTING FLASHINGS

Flashings weatherproof the skylight installation, directing rain away from the inside of your home. But not all flashing is the same; different styles suit different types of roofing. Flashings for tile or heavy shake roofs differ somewhat from those for composition or wood shingle roofs. The same installation methods are usually used.

Some flashings are available ready-made. If you can't buy a suitable style, you can have flashing made at a sheet-metal shop. If you aren't sure what kind of flashing you need, the sheet-metal fabricator or a roofing contractor can help you decide. The technique for flashing a skylight curb is discussed on page 85.

All skylight flashings have two parts in common, the saddle flashings, which cover the top and bottom of the skylight curb, and also wrap partway around the sides. The upper piece is called the head flashing, and the lower piece is called the base or tail flashing.

SPECIAL ROOF FLASHINGS: Roofing materials that have irregular shape or thickness, such as tile, heavy shakes, or metal, requires special flashings. Head flashings for these high-profile roofing materials are the same as those used for shingle roofs. The flashing slips under the roofing material so it's not affected by the extra thickness. The base flashing, however, lies on top of the roofing, so it must conform to the roof surface closely to keep out wind and water. This is usually done with a corrugated soft lead flashing which can be easily worked by hand to conform to the contours of the roof. Tile and metal roofs usually need to have a continuous side flashing.

Lead works particularly well with tile. Use conventional or lead flashing with shake roofs, depending on how thick and irregular the shakes are and on how much the skylight is exposed to wind. Metal roofing comes in many patterns, and it is best to follow the manufacturer's recommendations for flashing a skylight on a metal roof.

Roof window manufacturers sometimes provide a U-shaped side flashing. The roofing rests on one leg of the U and the other leg runs up the side of the skylight. Water is carried away in the channel of the U. A thick soft-foam gasket promotes a good seal between the roofing and the corresponding leg of the U. A simple U-shaped side flashing can be made for a conventional skylight with a tile or shake roof.

SIDE FLASHINGS: You can use step flashing on the sides of the curb for most types of shingle roofing. Step flashings are interwoven with the shingles, so water that gets into the corner runs onto the top surface of the next shingle as it works its way down the roof.

For flat roofs, tar and gravel roofs, and those covered with roll roofing, a continuous L-shaped side flashing goes under the head flashing and over the base flashing. Never use an L-shaped flashing on a shingle roof.

Whatever type of flashing you use, buy it or have it made to fit the height of your skylight curb and the thickness of the roofing. The top edge of the flashing should come just below the top of the curb so that the lip of the skylight will overlap the flashing. If you are retrofitting a skylight to an existing roof, subtract the thickness of the roofing material from the height of the curb so that the flashing doesn't project up too high.

Be sure to use compatible nails with flashing. Use only copper nails with copper flashings, for example. Galvanic action between dissimilar metals will corrode through the nails or flashing.

FLASHING A SKYLIGHT CURB

Flashing won't work without proper overlap. Water always runs from one piece of flashing onto another as it flows down the roof. As you work up the side of the skylight curb, each step flashing overlaps the one below it and slips under the adjacent shingle. The uppermost edges of the base flashing go beneath the lowest pieces of step flashing. The sides of the head flashing overlap the highest step flashing, and the top edge of the head flashing lies under the roofing.

In windy locations, caulk or roofing cement will help prevent water from blowing up into the small joints between flashings. Sealants under the base flashing will help keep water and air from between it and the roofing.

If you are installing a skylight on an existing roof, you will need to lift shingles away from the roof to install the flashing.

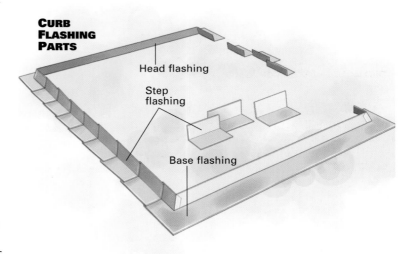

CURB FLASHING PARTS

Head flashing

Step flashing

Base flashing

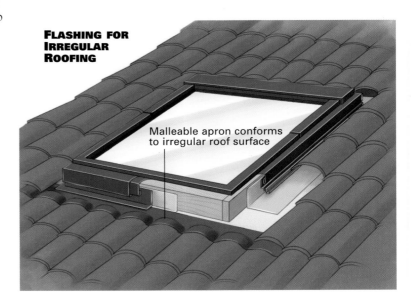

FLASHING FOR IRREGULAR ROOFING

Malleable apron conforms to irregular roof surface

INSTALLING A SKYLIGHT
continued

INSTALLING THE CURB

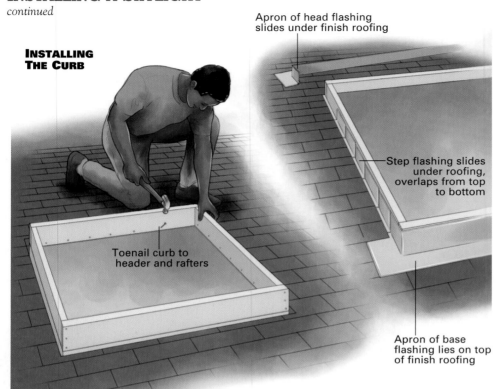

Apron of head flashing slides under finish roofing

Step flashing slides under roofing, overlaps from top to bottom

Toenail curb to header and rafters

Apron of base flashing lies on top of finish roofing

Work carefully to avoid breaking them; broken shingles can cause leaks. Composition shingles break easily in cold weather. If you must work on a cold day, try warming the shingle with a heat gun or hair dryer to soften it before you try to lift it.

The shingle may also be stuck to the one below it; they are designed to seal together to improve their wind resistance. Separate sealed-together shingles with a flat pry bar or a flexible putty knife.

■ To begin the installation, first fit the base flashing in a bed of caulk around the bottom edge of the curb. Note that the apron rests on top of the shingles along the bottom edge of the curb. This directs water over the shingles and off the roof. Don't place the apron beneath the shingles.

■ Nail the base flashing to the curb along the top edge of the flashing. Place the nails so that they will be covered by the skylight.

■ Fit the first piece of step flashing so that it overlaps the base flashing. Slide it beneath the adjacent shingle. Embed the edge next to the curb in caulk. Nail the flashing to the curb along the top edge.

■ You may also need to nail a piece of step flashing to the roof in order to make it lie flat. Do this only if you must; the fewer holes in the roof, the better. To nail the step flashing to the roof, gently lift up a shingle and nail the flashing so that the shingle will cover the nail. If you can't swing the hammer because the shingle is in the way, hold a heavy, flat pry bar on the nail and strike it just below the edge of the shingle. That should drive the nail, leaving the shingle undamaged.

■ Continue installing the step flashings on both sides until you reach the top of the curb.

■ Fit the head flashing around the top of the curb. Its apron must fit completely under the shingles. A common mistake is to get the edge under just one row of shingles so it's visible through the small gaps between the shingles. Those gaps will let water under the head flashing, creating leaks. Avoid the temptation to fill the gaps with caulk. It's best to work the flashing the rest of the way under two rows of shingles.

The usual difficulty in getting it all the way under the shingles is removing the shingle nails without destroying the shingles. One approach is to slip a flat pry bar under the shingle. Use a bar with a slight curve and a prying notch in the long end. Catch the nail with the notch and pry it out.

■ Patch any holes or broken shingles with caulk or roofing cement after the job is done.

INSTALLING A CURB-MOUNTED SKYLIGHT

■ Set the curb over the opening and double-check to ensure that it is centered and square. Then toenail it from the inside through the roof and deck into the rafters and headers.

■ Install the flashing (see page 85). Apply a bead of caulk or resilient weather stripping to the top of the skylight curb.

■ Drop the skylight over the curb and flashing. Nail it to the curb along the upper edge or through the factory-drilled holes. Cover each nail head with a dab of caulk or roofing cement.

CUTTING THE LIGHT WELL OPENING

With the skylight in place, you can open the ceiling and finish the light well without worrying about rain.

■ You can frame the ceiling opening before you cut the opening in the ceiling. Support the ceiling joists in the attic by laying two 2×4s flat across the joists 2 feet back from the planned opening. They should reach two rafters beyond the last rafter to be cut on each side. Drill holes through the 2×4s and into the top of each joist; then fasten them with 4-inch screws.

■ Frame the ceiling opening, following the same procedure you used to frame the roof opening. (See page 83.)

■ When the framing is complete, cut out the ceiling opening by punching a wallboard saw through the ceiling from above and cutting along the edge of the framing material. Have someone below support the cutout.

Caulking

Apron of base
flashing lies on top
of finish roofing

INSTALLING A SKYLIGHT

continued

CONSTRUCTING THE LIGHT WELL

Frame the light well with 2×4s, spaced not more than 24 inches apart on center, between the rafters and ceiling joists.

■ If your light well slants from the skylight to the ceiling opening, you must cut the top and bottom of the 2×4s to the correct angle. To determine the angle easily, cut a 2×4 a couple of inches less than the measured distance from the roof deck to the ceiling at roughly the desired angle. Place it against the rafters and joists at the precise angle. Then mark the 2×4 where it crosses the rafter and joist, as shown below. Cut the angles on the ends, and set the 2×4 aside as an angle template.

■ If you have installed a skylight with jack rafters and jack joists, the roof and ceiling openings should line up directly from side to side. In this case, you can cut the 2×4s to

length, then toenail the tops of the 2×4s to the rafters and the bottoms to the joists.

■ However, if your skylight fits against an existing rafter and your light-well opening is against an existing joist, you will have a problem. Because the ceiling joists are nailed to the sides of the rafters where they meet on the cap plate of the stud wall, they are not lined up directly. To frame straight sides for the light well in this case, nail the 2×4s on one side to the face of a joist and toenail them to the bottom edge of a rafter. On the other side of the light well, nail the 2×4s to the face of the rafter and toenail them to the top of the joist.

■ Nail another 2×4 on the back edge of the each corner support to provide a nailing surface for the wallboard.

■ Staple insulation bats around the light well with the foil facing into the well.

■ Finish the light well by covering the interior with drywall or paneling.

Provide temporary support for the ceiling joists before cutting the ceiling opening. Lag-screw 2×4s to the joists 2 feet beyond the proposed cut.

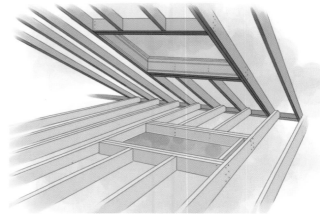

Frame the ceiling opening with a doubled header on each end and a trimmer at each side of the opening. Install the framing before cutting through the ceiling.

If the roof opening is offset from the ceiling opening, align a piece of 2×4 with the same corner in each opening. Mark the top and bottom angles on the 2×4.

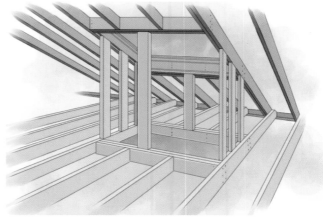

Install the framing members for the walls of the light well. Add blocking to the corner studs to provide nailing surfaces for the drywall corners.

TRIMMING SKYLIGHTS

Skylights can be trimmed in almost any manner, depending on whether you want to focus on the skylight itself or on the light that it admits into the room.

If you want to draw attention to a single area by flooding it with light, use unobtrusive skylight trim. Elaborate trim will emphasize the skylight itself or the light well. If there is a light well, you must decide if you want to trim it out. Usually a light well is just finished off in wallboard or plaster, with the surface painted a pale color so that light entering the well reflects into the room. Most skylights are designed so that the wallboard can run right up against the bottom edge. In this case, no further trim is required. You may need to shim one or more of the walls of the well to ensure that the wallboard meets all the edges of the skylight evenly.

An alternative to wallboard or plaster is to line the light well with wood paneling or trim. Follow the techniques used for trimming the side jambs of windows. (See page 58.) Finish the job with a flat piece of trim resting on the edge of the side jamb and on the surface of the roof. Or install a narrow trim band where the wallboard meets the skylight unit.

You can trim a light well with casing to match the doors and windows in the room (above), or finish it as part of the ceiling (right).

SEALING THE HOUSE

Newer doors and windows have well-engineered weather-sealing systems that minimize drafts. Older doors and windows in a home, however, may not be so weathertight. Hardware stores and home centers sell a number of weather-stripping products (see some examples on these two pages) that can help you exclude drafts.

CAULKING

Don't overlook the value of caulking in eliminating drafts. Inspect the caulking around the exterior trim on windows and doors. Where there are gaps, scrape out the old caulking and apply new. Rope caulking will seal wider gaps. Another way to close large gaps is to press a foam backing rod into the gap, then caulk over it. The rod is available in several diameters at hardware stores and home centers.

WEATHER-STRIPPING A DOOR

To seal an exterior door against drafts, first make sure the door fits its opening correctly and that the stops are all in place.

Tighten hinge screws or replace the hinges, if needed. Plane the door as necessary so it closes solidly against the stops.

Next install metal or plastic weather stripping on the jamb sides and head, as shown in the illustration on page 92. Make sure the gap between the door and the jamb is wide enough for the weather stripping before you nail it into place.

If the tension strip weather stripping won't work for your door, install a bulb-type gasket. To install it, close the door. Then cut the pieces to length, press the bulb against the face of the door, and nail or screw the weather stripping to the door stop.

At the bottom of the door, install either a door sweep or a door shoe with a vinyl insert to seal against the threshold. Another choice is to install a threshold with a bulb insert, which will work with a plain door bottom.

Felt Strip
Made of hair, wool, or synthetic fibers; tack, staple, or glue in place; not good for exterior exposure

Flange Stripping
Made of vinyl or rubber; bulb presses against the surface to be sealed; often available with a plastic or aluminum flange

Threshold with Insert
Made of aluminum and vinyl; the bulb insert seals against bottom of door for a good seal; door must fit well; various heights are available for different floors

Foam Tape
Made of polyurethane or vinyl; self-adhesive, presses in place; install as a gasket

Sponge Rubber
Made of rubber, harder and more durable than foam tape; usually self-adhesive

Door Shoe
Made of aluminum and vinyl; attaches to face of door, covers bottom; provides drip cap and bottom gasket; effective even in harsh climates

Bristle Sweep
Made of aluminum or vinyl with nylon bristles; works well on sliding doors; screws to face of door

Tension Strip
Made of metal or vinyl; effective and long-lasting; vinyl is often self-adhesive; requires well-fitting door or window for best seal

Door Sweep
Made of vinyl or aluminum and vinyl; attaches to face of door; provides an effective seal against a threshold; automatic type raises to clear carpeting when the door is opened

SEALING THE HOUSE

continued

WEATHER-STRIPPING DOORS

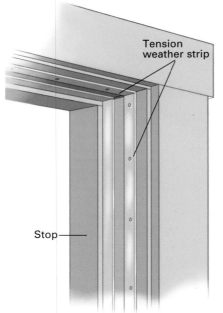
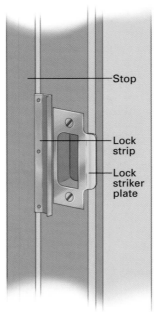

Tension weather strip

Stop

Stop

Lock strip

Lock striker plate

AUTOMATIC DOOR SWEEP

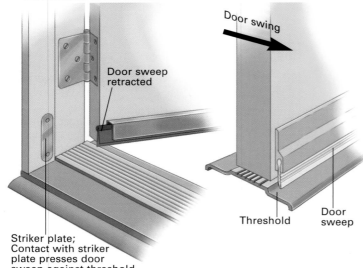

Door sweep retracted

Door swing

Striker plate; Contact with striker plate presses door sweep against threshold

Threshold

Door sweep

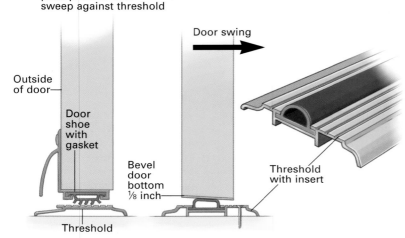

Door swing

Outside of door

Door shoe with gasket

Bevel door bottom ⅛ inch

Threshold with insert

Threshold

WEATHER-STRIPPING WINDOWS

You can weather-strip windows several ways. The type of window—double-hung, casement, or awning—and the material it's made of are factors to consider. Jalousie windows, for instance, are difficult to weatherproof, and fixed-pane windows and skylights usually need only caulking to keep out drafts.

Here are some general guidelines; but you should follow the installation instructions provided by the manufacturer of the weather stripping you select.

The double-hung sash with metal tension stripping in the illustration at right shows the principles of weather-stripping a window. Here's how to do it:

■ Measure strips to fit the side channels for both sashes, as well as the upper rail of the top sash, the lower rail of the bottom sash, and the lower rail of the top sash. Cut the strips to length with tin snips.

■ Slide the side channel strips into place between the sashes and jambs and nail them in place.

■ Slide the upper-rail, top-sash strip into the top channel of the window and the lower-rail, bottom-sash strip into the bottom channel. Nail them in place. Or you can nail the upper-rail, top-sash strip to the upper side of the top sash and the lower-rail bottom-sash strip to the underside of the bottom sash.

■ Nail the last strip to the inside surface of the lower rail of the top sash (the center bar). If the strips don't fit tightly enough, you can pry out the side-channel flanges with a screwdriver or a putty knife.

■ Drive all nails flush to prevent snagging.

SLIDING WINDOW: Treat a sliding window the same way as a double-hung window—just imagine that it's lying on its side. If only one sash slides, use metal tension stripping in the channel that opens; seal the three remaining edges of the movable sash with tubular flange stripping to create a good seal all the way around.

CASEMENT WINDOW: For a wood casement window or any kind of tilting window, such as an awning or a hopper, nail the weather stripping to the frame with the flange along the edge toward which the window opens. For a metal casement window, buy a deeply grooved gasket stripping that fits over the metal edges of the window frame, available at most hardware stores or home centers. To make the stripping hold well, first apply rubber/metal or vinyl/metal glue on the edge of the frame or the gasket channel.

ALTERNATE METHODS

Here's how to install some other types of weather stripping:

FLANGE STRIPPING: You can nail, staple, or screw vinyl or rubber flange-type weather stripping all around the sash. Nail it to the outside of the window frame to make it less visible, when possible. It should fit tightly on all surfaces, inside or out, including the lower rail of the top sash.

Nail gasket stripping to the window frame with the thick or bulbous side against the sash. Make sure that the rolled edges fit tightly against the window when it's closed. Then add stripping to the lower rail of the top sash (the center bar) on the inside edge to make a tight seal between the sashes when the whole window is closed.

FOAM TAPE AND SPONGE RUBBER: Any adhesive-backed stripping can simply be pressed into place with your fingers. Clean the surface so the tape will adhere. Then apply the stripping, slowly pulling off the paper or plastic backing as you go. Do not use this weather stripping where it will be subject to friction, for example in side channels. It will wear out quickly or pull off.

FELT STRIPPING: You can either staple felt in place with an ordinary heavy-duty staple gun or nail it to the window frame like gasket stripping. Add a length of felt to the inside of the lower rail of the top sash so air won't get between the sashes.

Don't attach felt stripping to the outside of a window; if it gets wet, it may rot. Like foam tape, felt should not be used where it will be subjected to friction.

WEATHER-STRIPPING WINDOWS

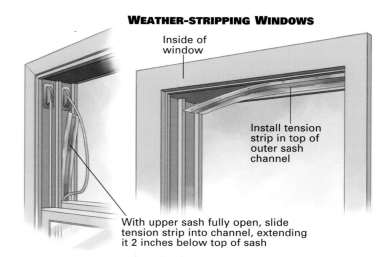

Inside of window

Install tension strip in top of outer sash channel

With upper sash fully open, slide tension strip into channel, extending it 2 inches below top of sash

Nail tension strip to sill, with inside edge against stool

With lower sash open, slide tension strip into channel, extending it 2 inches above bottom of sash

CASEMENT WINDOWS

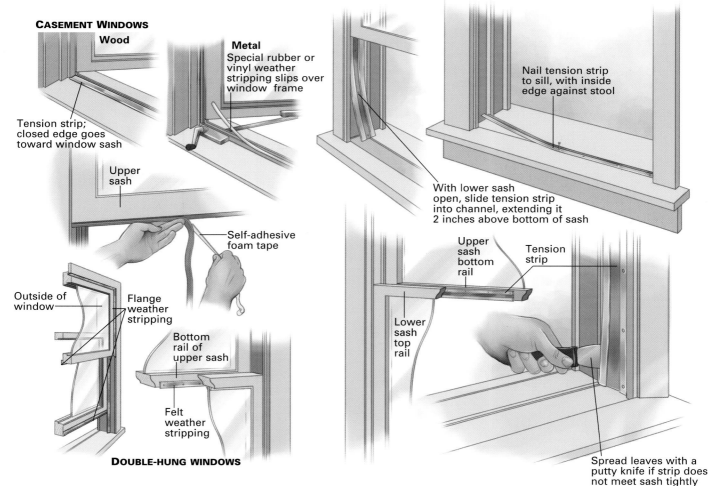

Wood

Metal
Special rubber or vinyl weather stripping slips over window frame

Tension strip; closed edge goes toward window sash

Upper sash

Self-adhesive foam tape

Outside of window

Flange weather stripping

Bottom rail of upper sash

Felt weather stripping

DOUBLE-HUNG WINDOWS

Upper sash bottom rail

Tension strip

Lower sash top rail

Spread leaves with a putty knife if strip does not meet sash tightly

INDEX

METRIC CONVERSIONS

U.S. Units to Metric Equivalents			Metric Units to U.S. Equivalents		
To Convert From	Multiply By	To Get	To Convert From	Multiply By	To Get
Inches	25.4	Millimeters	Millimeters	0.0394	Inches
Inches	2.54	Centimeters	Centimeters	0.3937	Inches
Feet	30.48	Centimeters	Centimeters	0.0328	Feet
Feet	0.3048	Meters	Meters	3.2808	Feet
Yards	0.9144	Meters	Meters	1.0936	Yards
Square inches	6.4516	Square centimeters	Square centimeters	0.1550	Square inches
Square feet	0.0929	Square meters	Square meters	10.764	Square feet
Square yards	0.8361	Square meters	Square meters	1.1960	Square yards
Acres	0.4047	Hectares	Hectares	2.4711	Acres
Cubic inches	16.387	Cubic centimeters	Cubic centimeters	0.0610	Cubic inches
Cubic feet	0.0283	Cubic meters	Cubic meters	35.315	Cubic feet
Cubic feet	28.316	Liters	Liters	0.0353	Cubic feet
Cubic yards	0.7646	Cubic meters	Cubic meters	1.308	Cubic yards
Cubic yards	764.55	Liters	Liters	0.0013	Cubic yards

To convert from degrees Fahrenheit (F) to degrees Celsius (C), first subtract 32, then multiply by ⅝.

To convert from degrees Celsius to degrees Fahrenheit, multiply by ⅖, then add 32.